ARCTIC

OCEAN

NORTH
AMERICA

PACIFIC

OCEAN

SOUTH
AMERICA

NEW ZEALAND

CHILE

VALDIVIA

--- The Journey of James Porter and his fellow
ship thieves from Macquarie Harbour to Chile

—— James Porter was twice transported from
Portsmouth to Van Diemen's Land

The Ship Thieves

The Ship Thieves

SIÂN REES

Aurum

For the boys: Joaquín, Nicolas and Felix

Contents

1

The Chain Gang

One midsummer night in 1829, James Porter looked furtively for the guard, took a stolen file from beneath his jacket and set it to the rings around his legs. He had been shackled to a chain gang for six months, ever since he was sent up from Hobart Town to break and lay stone in a line of twice- and thrice-convicted felons. Fifteen years later, he would recall that labour camp as 'one of the most dreadful places I have ever seen'.

From sunset to sunrise, Porter and the other prisoners were locked into huts so small that 'the whole number [could] neither stand upright nor sit down at the same time [except with their legs at right angles to their bodies], and which, in some instances, do not allow more than 18 inches in width for each individual to lie down upon on the bare boards'. At half-past five each morning, they were called to muster and marched to the quarries. After three hours of breaking stone, they were given a pint of skilly, a 'hasty pudding composed of flour, water and salt', and a slice of bread. 'I have to overlook them,' wrote a boastful young soldier to his mother at home in England, 'with a stick in my hand and . . . I am obliged to be very severe with them. If I report any of them for neglect, they get 25 to

50 lashes.' Every day, lunch was mutton and potatoes, and if an overseer fancied the food in a man's bowl for himself or his favourite, that man was wise to say nothing. Once all were fed, the guards leant again on their muskets and watched, and more stone was deafeningly broken and laid by men hacking passes through the rock. Each convict wore the hated iron bar between his legs and slops patched with the incongruous harlequin colours of yellow and blue; each was chained to the next. When they returned to camp at the end of the day, more skilly was sent to the cells, bolts were drawn and the prisoners were left caged and unattended. What happened by night among men already 'degraded and incorrigible', was not part of the soldier's watch. The chain gang, said the colonial governor who had devised the system, was 'as severe a punishment as can be inflicted'. The prospect of three years here was too much for James Porter. He was determined 'to escape this scene of wretchedness or perish in the attempt'.

The camp was in Van Diemen's Land, now known as Tasmania, thirteen thousand miles and four months' sailing from London, and Porter's escape plan was the same as that of fugitives all over the island: to steal a small boat, head downriver for the coast and sell his labour to some ocean-bound skipper. Small craft littered the banks and creeks of the River Derwent, close to the chain-gang camp: punts, barges, gigs, cutters of shallow draft and the ubiquitous whaleboat which, in this mountainous, unexplored island, would connect the coastal townships until the roads were cut through rock and laid. A day's sailing from the Derwent estuary would take him close to the whalers and sealers of a dozen nationalities who had colonised the island's east and south coasts. These were the hard men of the sea, who cared nothing for the judges of Hobart, nor the policies of London, nor anything but gain and gratification. They kept Aboriginal women chained to huts for their use and turned out blinding liquors from their distilleries. Here, it was hoped, were captains who might welcome runaway convicts begging to work their passage out, the women on their backs and the men before the mast, carrying the valuable whale oil to ports across the world.

Selecting four or five of his fellow prisoners to man a stolen whaleboat's oars and row quietly away downriver, James Porter 'put the question to them, they agreed and the Saturday came we were to seize the sentry and overseers and fly from slavery'. It was only when he was too far compromised to change his mind, with the iron rings loosened and fallen about his ankles, that Porter found the men who had promised to accompany him had changed theirs. They were timid, or exhausted, or unsure of their captain's skill. They preferred to work out their existing second sentence to risking a third for a failed escape. James Porter would have to go alone, and fast, for the alarm would soon be given by some scheming comrade, hungry for an informer's reward. Should he be found with a file and a broken chain between his ankles, he would be lashed to the triangles and flogged, his sentence would be lengthened, his irons doubled and his rations reduced. Free from his shackles, he crept to the perimeter of the camp, pushed a sleepy guard into a ditch and pelted into the night.

James Porter had already spent five years on Van Diemen's Land, sent by London to this lush, corrupt island outpost of the great Australian gaol that hung in the Pacific above them. A fragile settlement had been established here in 1803, when a tiny group of Europeans came across the Bass Straits from New South Wales to protect it from the Americans, who plundered its fisheries, and the French, who threatened to plant the tricolour on its beaches. A village emerged from their tents, pitched between the waters of the Derwent and the slopes of Mount Wellington. This was Hobart Town, or 'Hobarton', the disturbed southern offspring of Sydney Cove.

Its infancy was dominated by hunger, assuaged by scraping seaweed from the rocks and scouring the beaches for burnt blubber discarded by American whalers round the coast, who watched the British flounder and starve, and kept themselves apart.

The first Vandemonians survived by the distribution of guns and the massacre of kangaroos, beating back the bush and its people in their hunt. From this early, easy bloodshed, a culture of violence was born. When supply-ships from London and Sydney began to call and an influx of convict labour began to coax crops from the island's soil, few islanders returned their guns to the Hobart pound. Convict roo-shooters preferred the independence of the bush to labouring on a settler's farm and stayed out. They pushed further inland and began shooting the blacks, first in competition for meat and skins; then for sport; later, as part of a government policy that ended in the extinction of a race. 'Here,' wrote a tired official in 1810, when the colony was just seven years old, 'wickedness flourishes unchecked.'

It flourished further. Lieutenant-Governor 'Mad Tom' Davey, a Devonshire boy turned soldier, was drunk when he came ashore and rarely sobered in a four-year regime. He ruled by use of rum and rope and passed a colony in chaos to Lieutenant-Governor William Sorell when that able gentleman arrived to replace him, accompanied by a lady who was not his wife. Sorell inherited turmoil: where the *banditti* did not rule, the angry blacks did. Settlers were armed and afraid. Administration was chaotic: no one knew how many convicts were on the island, where they were and for whom they were working, what their conduct had been, how much time they had left to serve, nor even the crimes for which they had been sent here or for how long. Sorell cleaned up some of Mad Tom's mess and broke the bushranging gangs, ignoring sour comments about his companion, the rum-parties held in the rackety salons of Government House and the gaggle of little bastards in its bedrooms.

His plans were sound and his seven years efficient, but Van Diemen's Land continued a 'hard and inhospitable place'; home, wrote a disenchanted visitor, to 'the flotsam and jetsam of the world, men seeking refuge from the law or seeking isolation from other human beings . . . rough frontiersmen [who] despoiled and exploited everything and everyone they saw . . .'

All this Lieutenant-Governor Sir George Arthur knew and was determined to change when he disembarked the *Adrian* in Hobart Town on 12 May 1824, dressed in the uniform of a colonel, with his children and prim wife Eliza behind him, their bibles, plain gowns, evangelical tracts, family organ and the other furniture of a pious life being brought up from the hold. Arthur had come from governorship of the slave state of British Honduras and he was of a different clay to the drunk and the adulterer who had both slept in the big bed of Government House before him. He was straight-backed, straitlaced, teetotal, unsmiling, untiring; an indefatigable administrator with a mania for detail. He had heard the word of God in Honduras. In Van Diemen's Land, this would be passed on as the word of Arthur. He would introduce discipline and morality to his wayward fiefdom, wrapped up in a system of complete control: mechanical, incorruptible, self-regulating—the perfect gaol. He called it 'enlightened rigour'.

Governor Arthur established a network of Police Magistrates, through whose hands power would be channelled. He developed and enforced William Sorell's system of punishment and rehabilitation, determining seven rigid levels of Vandemonian convicthood, from ticket of leave (limited emancipation) at level one, to which all must aspire if the system were to function; graded down to hard labour in an isolated penal settlement, in chains, at level seven, to which degradation and pain all must dread descending. To chart his convicts' rise and fall, Arthur commanded the creation of 'Black

Books', great registers designed to suck in every scrap of scattered information about them: offence, place of trial, sentence, colour of hair and eyes, tattoos, occupation, father's occupation, skills, age, marriage, children, 'indulgences' applied for and those given, medical reports and secondary offences, all inscribed below his or her name until death, departure or emancipation.

James Porter had arrived in Van Diemen's Land four months before Sir George. In 1823, down on his luck, he committed a clumsy burglary in Kingston-on-Thames, near London, and went before the Surrey justices. He was not considered suitable material for mercy. They sentenced him to transportation for the term of his natural life. He arrived in Hobart Town aboard the *Asia* with 249 other men, packed and stacked on the bottom deck for four months, two days' sailing and shuffled whey-faced and blinking into the island's diamond light on 11 January 1824. He and his shipmates were to be the raw material for the new governor's schemes and records, the faces and flesh behind the names in his Black Books, the servants of his settlers and the backs which carried the stones for his public works.

While Lieutenant-Governor Arthur set out to impose his Christian autocracy, James Porter and his mates set out to subvert it, although they would never have given their amusements such a grand name as subversion. It was larking, gammoning, skiving, rooking or pulling a fast one. It was being flash; it was getting away with as little work as possible; avoiding the police who hauled a man in for gambling or drinking; making a little money on the side when you could and sneaking out of barracks after curfew. James Porter was adept at all this. He did not particularly stand out; he was quick with his fists and impulsive but had sharp enough wits for an alehouse crowd and a notable ability to climb fresh-smelling from his messes, leaving unluckier others to take the blame.

Porter had begun his tricks on the day the *Asia* was piloted between the heads of the River Derwent and brought to anchor off Signal Mount, Hobart Town. The Muster Master came aboard with his papers and quills and convict clerks and the prisoners were lined up on deck to answer his questions. Had they been treated well on the voyage? Had they anything to report? One by one, they stepped forward to receive their colonial identity.

Newly christened Police Number 324 gave his name as Porter, James; his age as nineteen (he lied, he was in his mid-twenties); his place of birth as 'Bermondsey, London'; his most recent address as the Elephant and Castle in south London; and his father's occupation as 'weigher at the Custom House'. He was measured, and his height recorded as five foot two inches (small, but not remarkably so for his time); inspected, and noted as blind in the left eye, with brown eyes and hair, a dimpled chin and scars on forehead and neck; stripped to the waist, and found to be tattooed with two bare-fist boxers on his left arm. He was then asked his occupation and replied *beer machine maker* while his shipmates chortled. There is no such occupation. It was a joke and a provocation, the response of a cocky little man to authority.

Most of the *Asia* men were, like James Porter, malnourished townies, bred to the life of the urban drifter: casual labour and petty crime. Disembarked, they waited in Hobart gaol for assignation to their new masters, the free men—and a very few women—who had been granted land and convict labour to develop the Crown's territory. They hoped not to be sent to a 'dungaree settler' in the bush 'to work from sun to sun on short commons', for they needed clamour and bustle and feared an endless sky and silence. Knowing only those who professed urban trades would find an urban master, James Porter was ready with a dodge and a dive, wangling a place at a Hobart smithy. A first test at the anvil immediately exposed him as a fraud. The initial terse entry in the name of *Porter, James* came only two months after he stepped off the *Asia*. Others soon followed. In March 1824, he was accused of 'stealing butter and having no lodgings'. The charge of theft did not stick but no convict could be allowed to wander the streets at night. He was sent to the Public Barracks to await assignment to Public Works. This demotion through the system was insufficient to knock the cockiness out of Porter. A month later, he escaped. Had the colonial authorities known a little more of his history than the few bare facts recorded by the Muster Master, they might have realised it was inevitable, for Police Number 324 was an inveterate bolter.

From his own telling of it, James Porter's youth had been a ramshackle and reckless affair. He had first gone to sea aged twelve or thirteen, aboard an uncle's brig, press-ganged by his own family, he would claim, for stealing from his grandmother. Treated too strictly for his liking by the officers—'mastheaded on the most trivial occasion'—he jumped ship in Rio de Janeiro, taking with him 100 dollars and 50 doubloons of the captain's money, and returned to England. On a second voyage to South America, he got as far as Valparaiso on the coast of Chile, then 'stealing from the purser's stores, swayed away on the slop chest and . . . having a good bit of money about me,' again 'bid farewell to the ship', persuading 'a Spanish girl [to stow] me away on her father's premises until the ship sailed again'. This obliging young lady, Narcisa, soon became Señora de Porter. She brought a farm to the union as dowry, bore a son and was deserted two years later when 'an inclination to go to sea for a trip or two' came over her swain and he bolted again. On shore leave in Callao, he got mixed up in a grog-shop brawl, killed a local man and was hidden away on a London-bound ship by sympathetic bluejackets. 'Stung with remorse', he recalled, at leaving his family alone and unprotected, Porter nevertheless enjoyed the 'stiff breeze in our favor' and thoughts of England. In London, having blown the wages that might have paid his passage back to Narcisa, he committed the burglary for which he was arrested, sentenced and transported to Van Diemen's Land.

On 4 May 1824, four months after his arrival, he climbed over a wall in Hobart Public Barracks and was out for eighteen days: holed up in some backstreet inn or hidden among the reeds of the river bank, spying the outgoing traffic for opportunity. By the time Porter came to write his memoirs seventeen years later, he had tried to escape too many times, and in too many places, to remember the details of this early attempt. On 22 May the guards brought him in, tied him to the triangle and flogged him one hundred times.

With his back still raw and sore, Porter was sent to the 'boat crew', joining the gangs of seamen convicts who worked the government brigs *Tamar, Opossum* and *Prince Leopold* under the command of Captain Welsh in Hobart harbour. A man with several years' experience before the mast was a useful acquisition for a busy harbour master and Porter found a niche in which, for a couple of years, he managed to stay out of trouble and earn his employer's esteem. His life in Hobart harbour was not dissimilar to that of any free seaman signed up to a merchantman or naval vessel: strict discipline, strict obedience to orders but also companionship and some of the self-respect that comes from practising a skilled trade. There was even time ashore in semi-freedom, where sailors in the convict rig were part of the Hobart mix, along with the silent, half-naked blacks who came in from the bush to stand and watch in the streets, and the old-timers who still called the town 'camp': kangaroo-men dressed in sheepskin moccasins and a stinking frock-coat of kangaroo skins, tailed by their packs of dogs; settlers in from Huon and Freycinet, their mule carts laden with produce; and bored soldiers waiting to go home. Then something went wrong on the boat crew, for in August 1826 James Porter bolted again. This time, he was out only 24 hours before the guards found him hiding on board the *Sydney* packet boat and the magistrates charged him with 'intent to escape from the colony'.

James Porter was but one of many convicts determined to free himself from penal servitude. Convicts had been stealing small boats and heading for the oceans since the earliest days of Australian settlement. There were British fugitives in the Bass Straits and New Zealand's Bay of Islands; communities of feral, hungry whites were strung along the unexplored coasts of mainland Australia and small islands across the Pacific housed lean, lonely Britons, put ashore by angry or indifferent captains to make the best of it. Most did not get even this far: they drowned, or were chased and caught; or returned, more frightened by the elements and empty horizons than they were by guards and the lash.

As the Australian colonies became trading posts as well as gaols, more ships began to call at their ports. In the 1820s, when the River Derwent was still so 'filled with beastly whales it was dangerous to make a crossing', Hobart had come to dominate the global whaling trade, with as many as 50 ocean-going whalers fitting out at any one time in the harbour, scores of smaller craft cruising coastal waters in search of sperm whales and merchantmen bringing in supplies to tempt a young and cash-rich society. This increase in shipping had predictable results. The more ambitious fugitives turned their attention from cutters and launches to the larger vessels new to the harbours, built and rigged for ocean sailing. In 1811, the first privately owned schooner to trade regularly between Van Diemen's Land and New South Wales was hijacked in the River Derwent and never seen again. In 1819, the captain of the *Young Lachlan* ignored regulations, anchoring off Macquarie Point with rudder and sails attached. Convicts climbed aboard, drifted downriver, raised her sails and made for Java, where they ran her ashore and set fire to her. In 1820, other convicts took the *Governor Sorell*; in 1822, the *Sea Flower*; in 1825, the *Blue-Eyed Maid*; then came illicit flight aboard the *Despatch*, the *Helen*, the *Cyprus* and the *Shannon*.

From his arrival, Governor Arthur had struggled endlessly to block the escape routes but Van Diemen's Land, with its long, unexplored coasts, was a leaky vessel. His roads and lists and magistrates might subdue the interior but seaborne traffic was more slippery. All smaller ships coming into Hobart were ordered to detach sails and rudders and bring them ashore. Every ship anchored in the River Derwent was required to mount a 24-hour officer watch. Every ship due to leave was fumigated with sulphur to force any stowaways on deck. If a convict were found on board, every man and officer was fined a month's wages and the ship did not sail until the fines were paid. Informers were rewarded and protected. Despite these precautions, dozens each year still wriggled through the wall of smoke and sentries and got away, aboard whalers to work the long, hard passage to America, if nothing better offered itself; but if cunning could contrive it, hidden aboard vessels bound for the Cape, Rio and Europe.

For James Porter's second failed escape, he was sentenced to six months on a chain gang, level five of Arthur's system. This sentence was cut short, apparently on the recommendation of the patient Captain Welsh, who needed skilled seamen in an increasingly busy port. By January 1827, Porter was back in Hobart harbour aboard the *Prince Leopold* but some bitterness or stubborn determination seems to have set in. The Porter entries in the Black Book began to come more frequently: one charge of stealing a boat and two oars, another of 'robbing one of the sailors belonging to the *Sir Charles Forbes*'. The first resulted in an acquittal, the second was dismissed for want of evidence but they indicate at the least bad company and at the most a crime well committed. On 24 July of that year, he came before a magistrate for the third time in six months.

Private Henry Kelly had been guarding a bonded warehouse on the Hobart wharf when two drunks staggered towards him and collapsed. Kelly recognised them as 'convict seamen' who worked for Captain Welsh and asked them what they were doing. Captain Welsh had given them permission to stay out until 'near nine if they liked', they said, and, when Kelly ordered them to stand, they told him to 'bugger himself'. He fixed his bayonet. They threatened he would have '300 lashes on his back for breakfast'. Both men spent that night in the watchhouse. The following morning, the court deliberated and sentenced one of them to 25 lashes. The other, whom Captain Welsh had again 'given a favourable character', was let off with a reprimand. James Porter had wriggled free again but his conduct record was lengthening and this was what Governor Arthur would consult when any request for an 'indulgence' was made. Every negative entry in the book put back the time when a convict could work a few hours for himself, then a few more, then days and finally weeks; when he could ask a woman to marry him, own property, start a family, gain a ticket of leave and be free. For the hundreds like James Porter who could not stay out of trouble, however petty, emancipation did not inexorably approach, as Arthur's system was designed to ensure; rather, with equal inexorability, it receded.

In March 1828, absences without leave were recorded again, with reprimands; then, in June, a charge of 'making use of the government boat to his own private advantage contrary to orders and with taking men down the river without proper authority'. This implied another escape attempt, and had to be flogged out of him. Another 25 lashes only flogged the recalcitrance in. Six months later, Porter was charged with felony: 'stealing 70 boards value £2 property of the King'. It was not his fault, he would later claim: a fellow seaman who 'only wanted 10 days to do out of 14 years' stole planks to make a seachest and was arrested 'nearly broken-hearted, and asked me if there was any chance of his being saved. I said none except for me to take it on myself. I consented to get convicted if he would promise to have a whaleboat ready when I got sent to a Chain Gang . . . he promised he would . . .' and so James Porter, at least in his own version, took the blame and nobly went to the chain gang in the place of his mate.

It was for this offence, whoever committed it, and from which Captain Welsh could not or would not save him, that Porter found himself swinging his axe, clad in the yellow jacket that showed the recidivist up against the bush. The whaleboat had not come, if it had ever been promised—if indeed, the seaman who promised it had ever existed. Thus, one brightly lit midsummer night, James Porter cursed his pusillanimous mates and struck out alone for the river.

Outside the camp perimeter, he had still to elude the guards whose half-wild dogs, alerted by the bruised and angry sentry, had been set on his trail. 'I had just sufficient time,' he recalled, 'to lash the rings of the irons to each leg,' and thus he leapt bushes, took ditches and reached the river with his pursuers close behind. Striking out downstream with the current, kicking against the irons that pulled his legs under, he was elated to see that none of the men piling up behind each other on the river bank was able to swim and follow him. The telltale, silent wake closed behind him and the river smoothed over. On the far side of Hobart Town, Porter hauled himself up a bank and thought he had lost the guards. He had not. As he looked about him for a break in the river-bank scrub, a boat appeared around the bend upstream. Recognising the men's voices, Porter again slipped into the river and tilted his head back until it scarcely broke the surface. Treading water with heavy legs, he waited until the boatload of sentries had passed and then began slowly, now against the current, to swim back the way he had come. Once he was level with the centre of Hobart, he pulled himself up the bank, ran dripping behind the gardens of Government House, where the Arthur family slept, and slipped into town. However, here, among the back streets and docks where he had spent most of the last five years, too many knew his face. 'I was recognised,' he recalled, 'and [fearing] a fresh pursuit might come on', gave his acquaintances the slip, exhausted but knowing he could not rest, crossed town and knocked on the door of one Mr Mansfield.

Mr Mansfield was a pilot: one of the skilled seamen who went out to visiting vessels to guide them along the channels of the Derwent estuary and into the harbour. As such, he was a well-known figure in the seafaring community and possibly acquainted with James Porter, a fellow seaman, if a convict one. Nevertheless, he must have been surprised to find the man swaying before his door, wet, cold and smelling of river mud. Mansfield did not enquire closely into his visitor's circumstances, only '[asking] me where I was going', Porter said. Porter claimed he had missed his vessel, the cutter on which he had previously worked. Perhaps Mr Mansfield had not heard of Porter's sentence to the chain gang, and accepted this explanation at face value; perhaps he knew exactly what Porter was up to, but was loyal to a seaman down on his luck. Either way, he 'ordered me supper and to sleep in his house that night'.

The Mansfields' house was small, and James Porter was shown into the same room as the family's two young sons, one of whom was woken and told to shift up so the stranger could climb in beside him. Most guests would have removed their sodden outer clothing but Porter could not, for this would reveal broken irons and confirm his secret. His unfortunate young host held back comment as the mattress grew damp and the blanket dirty but when Porter's trousers rode up his legs in sleep, jagged metal scratched the child and he crept out of his own bed and into his brother's. They conferred as the strange man slept; then took a candle and a match, approached the sleeping figure and pulled back the blanket. Porter woke to find his trousers knee-high and two faces transfixed by the rings lashed to his calves. He confessed that he was a runaway prisoner, wrongly and unjustly convicted, seeking his liberty. These two boys were either in love with adventure, thrilled by a runaway convict in their bed, or threatened with some vileness that Porter failed to mention in his memoirs. 'They pitied me,' was his explanation, 'and said they would not tell their father and for me to sleep and they would keep good watch for me and the Mastiff dog, so that no person could approach without notice.' Exhaustion, and trust in his two 'kind young protectors', led Porter again into a sleep from which the boys woke him at dawn and saw him on his way.

He crept through the early-morning streets and made for Signal Mount, where he hoped to find an empty dinghy to steal and row to Bruny Island, on the far side of the D'Entrecasteaux Channel. Only one soldier guarded the Mount, his mate having taken the buckets to draw the day's water, but he recognised the ill-shaven figure that sidled onto the beach just after dawn. Porter did not relate any words exchanged: only that the guard 'wanted to take me prisoner'. Whether the soldier declared this intention before he reached for his musket or whether the light of recognition in his eye was sufficient we can not know, but the fact remains; Porter reached for an axe and felled him before he could aim. Just then the second guard appeared with a yoke across his neck. Loath to tangle with another witness, Porter crouched and scrambled from view, not knowing when the man he left behind might come to and alert the authorities to a fresh trail. It was now too risky to make for one of the boats visible from Signal Mount. He would have to strike out through the bush for Oyster Cove, 20 miles to the west, and steal a boat there to make across the water to Bruny.

By boat, it would have been a short trip down the Derwent to Oyster Cove, past Battery Point, Sandy Bay, and the couple of whitewashed cottages on the headland where the men of the pilot's station watched the channel for approaching vessels and a few miles along the ocean coast. By foot, it was a different proposition, for the giant banyan scrub grew horizontally across the ground, and fern trees, several times the height of a man, were so dense that each frond had individually to be parted for the walker to climb through. Days in the bush were dark, for little sunlight pierced the canopy, and frightening, for leaves and webs clung to Porter's face and blinded his one good eye, boughs tripped and whipped him, gullies opened unexpectedly and the mud in their streams was thigh-deep and cold. This was country in which an experienced traveller might cover six miles a day, with axe and boots; a town-bred runaway, without either, would struggle to complete half that. With the first fern gully behind him, he was hidden but, by nightfall, he was also hopelessly lost.

Fuelled by optimism and accustomed to the chain-gang diet of gruel and water, Porter survived well enough the next day and second night. Even the second full day of dank green light and thrashing in hopeless circles did not bring hunger as much as frustration. But after the third night among the claustrophobic leaves, he 'felt the horrors of famishing'. Early on the morning of the fourth day, he was awoken by the barking of two dogs crashing through the undergrowth nearby in pursuit of a large kangaroo. Instantly alert, despite his fatigue, Porter's first thought was for security rather than sustenance. 'I expected to see the owner', he recalled, and froze, soundless, until this unknown person should come into view and reveal himself strong or small, armed or defenceless. As he waited, the dogs caught their prey not 50 yards away and began to rip the flesh from the corpse and feast. Still no one came to claim their prize. Porter rose, threatened the hounds until they slunk away to growl at a distance and 'took a hearty meal of the raw flesh and blood of the kangaroo'. The protein burst revived him. That evening, he stumbled out of the bush towards the light of a fire and the welcome of two Oyster Cove lime-burners.

He spent that night, his fifth on the run, bedded down in the lime-burners' hut, where he was finally able to break the remains of the irons from his legs. It was 'a happy releasement'. Newly mobile and newly rested, he was up at daybreak and on his way to the beach, seeking some empty and untended small boat that might take him across the strait to Bruny Island. But the constables of the Oyster Cove station hut were there before him, alerted perhaps by the man he had knocked unconscious at Signal Mount; perhaps more locally by the lime-burners, indifferent to the fate of last-night's guest, greedy for reward or afraid of prosecution for aiding a prisoner's escape. Porter saw them, dropped to the ground and amended his plan. The lime-burners' own boat rested on the strand and when the posse of Governor Arthur's men turned to inspect another part of the beach, he rushed it. His darting figure attracted their notice, he leapt the last yards under fire and, abandoning his attempt on the boat, 'sprung into the river, keeping under water as long as I could— the tide took me a great distance from my pursuers though not out of range of their muskets. I could hear the bullets fall into the water very close to me but did not receive any injury from them'.

Six days after leaving the chain gang, Porter finally washed up on a Bruny Island beach aboard a soft bed of floating kelp. That night, and the two following, he spent with an old acquaintance, now an assigned servant to one Mr Pybuss, who was away from home. On the ninth day of flight, news was brought to the visitor lying low in Mr Pybuss's barn that a vessel was in the bay, taking on oil, with *Port of London* written across her stern. This was news the visitor was happy to hear. Porter crossed the island. When the loading was done and while the crew were waiting for winds to haul away, he would make for the ship, stow away and wait until she was too far gone to turn back and off-load a runaway convict. London was in sight.

The wind faded with the light, then veered and strengthened, blowing straight into the mouth of the harbour where the London oil-ship was throwing out her anchors. Surf began to crash. The London vessel was out of reach until the wind dropped and Porter settled on the shingle to wait. All that night and most of the next day, the surf continued to batter the beach. It was still running high when the wind veered again and the London ship hauled her anchor and left. There was nothing to be done but return to Mr Pybuss's barn and wait.

Mr Pybuss, however, had returned from the mainland, and he knew James Porter, and knew James Porter was on the run. Governor Arthur's system of restraint might not prevent escape attempts but his system of detection and reward was more efficient. A government bounty on runaway convicts, payable to free and felon alike, invigorated good citizenship; bad was discouraged by the severe provisions of the *Harbouring Act*, which punished even the gift of food to strangers without informing the nearest constables of their presence. Names and particulars of missing convicts were published and posted up within hours of officials being notified of their flight and daily lists of these 'PRISONERS having absconded from their usual PLACES of RESIDENCE' were sent down newly laid roads to station huts across the island, with directions that 'all constables and others . . . use their utmost exertions to lodge them in safe custody'. It didn't take long for Mr Pybuss to earn himself a reward.

The following day, James Porter was aboard a cutter bound for Hobart Town, the authorities, the gaol and a heavier set of irons. However, in Porter's mind it was not quite over. As the cutter approached Seven Mile Point off the heads of Hobart, Porter leapt over the side. That night, he crawled ashore with renewed hope: another dinghy, another crossing to Bruny, another London oil-ship and freedom. None of this was impossible. He slept in exhaustion in the bed of a friend in Hobart Town and was arrested the following day, turned in by his host for the government's £40 reward.

This time, he was charged with being 'illegally at large under a Second Conviction'. In March 1830, he was sent in chains aboard his old ship, the *Prince Leopold*, bound for Macquarie Harbour.

2

A Place of Ultra Banishment

*I*n 1816, an open five-oared whaleboat left Hobart Town under the command of Captain James Kelly. It was less than 20 years since officers from Sydney had named and sailed the Bass Straits and discovered that this southern outpost was not a part of the Australian mainland. Much of the coast of Van Diemen's Land was still unmapped and unvisited. Battling into the Roaring Forties, which had deterred previous ships from landing on the wild west coast, Captain Kelly found a great, rain-soaked estuary, dark with spray and cloud, loud with a constant, shrieking wind. Waves rushed its entrance with the full, unimpeded force of the Southern Ocean behind them. Past the narrow mouth, an abundance of swans nested in the shallows and dripping virgin forests of Huon pine grew right down to the water's edge. The Gordon River tumbled in at the head, 30 miles inland, peat-brown and swollen by incessant rain. Kelly named this grim, magnificent place Macquarie Harbour, after the then Governor of New South Wales. On the estuary's southern shore he found swans, which, 'according to the barbarous custom adopted by some unfeeling individuals for the purpose of obtaining the down on the skins free from grease, [had] been penned up to starve', and released them. To mark this noble act Kelly called the spot Liberty Point and then sailed perilously out again, making for the islands of the Bass Straits, where feral colonies of sealers, wreckers and runaway convicts lived with their Aboriginal wives, whom they had bought for buttons, and their tribes of copper-skinned children.

A year after Captain Kelly's voyage, London ousted Mad Tom Davey from the governorship of Van Diemen's Land and sent William Sorell to replace him. One of Lieutenant-Governor Sorell's first projects was the establishment of a 'Place of Ultra Banishment and Punishment' for convicts who committed second offences during their term of penal servitude. He found the perfect location at Macquarie Harbour, for it was already rendered a gaol by geography. To the west, nature had provided the securest of sea-gates, narrow enough for a single patrol boat to guard and with a savage ocean beyond. To every other side, there was forest, then gullies of massive, tangled, impenetrable scrub, range after range of hills and finally mountains, iron-grey and veiled in cloud.

The first consignment of Macquarie Harbour convicts was sent up from Hobart Town in 1822, loaded into their boat without hammocks or bunks to sleep, if they could, among the stones of the ballast. They were regarded as the dregs of the colony: those for whom lighter sentences had not prevented reoffending; those who murdered; those who attacked their overseers; those who bolted into the bush and were recaptured after some short, violent career of rustling and rape. They were sent to the Harbour to repent and reflect as they worked waist-deep in icy water, logging the savage colonial pine. 'You must consider,' wrote Governor Sorell to the camp commandant, 'that the constant, active, unremitting employment of every individual in very hard labour is the grand and main design of your settlement. They must dread the very idea of being sent there.' Thus licensed for sadism, the first commandants made

Macquarie Harbour a truly hellish place. Hobart remained wilfully unaware of their entertainments, for the attitude of the colonial authorities towards the Harbour was like that of London towards the colony: there was disagreement as to whether it existed for reformation, punishment or empire-building but a unanimous disinclination to know the details of what went on there.

The *Prince Leopold* was due to take up supplies, dry goods and salt meat. James Porter was the only convict aboard. Labouring in the west coast's usual 'dreadful weather', the brig toiled north up a bleak white-water coastline, spiked with wrecks and sunken reefs. Sixteen days out from Hobart, first light found her tacking back and forth before the mouth of the estuary, drenched in spray, her canvas tight. The crew could not enter unaided, for 'Hell's Gates', the sardonic convict term for the harbour mouth, was, and is, one of the most dangerous harbour entrances in the world. Long sandbanks stretch out from the southern head to Entrance Island, two-thirds of the way across. Between the island and the northern head, the channel is just 50 yards wide and, twice in every 24 hours, a precarious eleven feet deep.

The Macquarie Harbour pilot, Mr Lucas, guarded his Gates like a hound, his boast that 'he had caught more runaways than he could count and did not mind what means he used to do it'. Inside the bar on the southern head, the flag went up on De Witts hill, behind a little row of huts that made up the 'pilot's establishment'. The sentry on cold, wet, solitary watch had seen the *Prince Leopold* and was signalling her arrival to the main settlement, 21 miles upriver. Shortly afterwards, Mr Lucas's boat came out to guide her in, manned by six convict oarsmen and one convict cox. Over the dangerous sandbar, the *Prince Leopold* was guided through calmer waters, passing vegetable gardens hacked from the bush on the southern shore, then two little islands, Betsey's Cap and Bonnet. Everywhere and everything was wet; every horizon was obscured by mist or spray, dull below cloud, only sparkling when the rare sun shone through. The whole place smelt of rotting vegetation and earth that was never dry.

Three miles up, they rounded Wellington Head, a promontory in whose lee sea-going vessels sheltered until wind and tide allowed them across the bar and through Hell's Gates. Shallow water opened up to the north, with tussocks of grass supporting the nests of swans, fewer now than in 1822, when bored officers had slaughtered them for sport. Liberty Point emerged from the salty fog, named for Captain Kelly's compassion, now an ironic comment on life in the estuary he discovered. Phillip Island loomed indistinctly, a 50-foot-high cliff facing seawards, with a plateau atop divided into potato plots. On the shore to either side grew the Huon pine, hard, bright and huge, with occasional clearings where the logging gangs had been at work. Five miles up from Phillip was the next of the estuary's islands, Sarah, named for a Hobart merchant's wife now surely horrified by the connection. When Captain Kelly came, Sarah Island had been thickly forested. Now most of the Harbour's population lived here and it was built over with barracks and the buildings of the penitentiary, workshops, officers' huts and stores, sawhouses, a bakery and a tannery. On the seaward shore, 30-foot-high lath fences had been convict-built, one just inside another like the defences of an ancient fort, to protect the huts and allotments from the ceaseless westerlies that rushed the river. As they approached the docks on Sarah's further shore, the howl of the wind gave way to the noise of work in the yards and the smell of foetid green to the scent of pine, freshly sawed and stacked in pungent piles. Officers and soldiers were awaiting their arrival, for a flag on De Witts hill was eagerly watched for by those stationed at this dim, dangerous post and brought any man not on duty to the docks in the hope of news, post, amusement—anything to break the monotony of the Harbour.

Macquarie Harbour may have been Governor Sorell's creation, but Governor Arthur had adopted and extended the experiment as he had other Sorellian schemes. 'Nothing I can imagine,' he wrote to the commandant he inherited, 'is more likely to lead to the Moral improvement of the most abandoned Characters in this Colony than a rigid course of discipline, strictly and systematically enforced . . . let your discipline be seasoned with Humanity, but never lose sight of the continued, rigid, unrelaxing discipline; and you must find Work and Labour, if it only consists of opening Cavities and filling them up again . . .'

Commandant Captain Briggs had not had to resort to ordering ditches dug and filled, for the Huon pine had provided sufficient hard labour for artifice to be unnecessary. Macquarie Harbour had become a logging camp and shipyard, supplying Hobart Town and Sydney with timber, furniture and boats. The governor's words had nevertheless been taken to heart: the work was performed with tools and techniques designed as much to weary their convict users as to render them efficient, in conditions that ensured the men were never sufficiently well-fed, dry or healthy to make labour easy. The stores aboard the *Prince Leopold* were destined for the 'commissariat', a group of timber-built huts on the wharf where all the apparatus and raw materials of chandlery and shipbuilding were stored: bolts of canvas, hundreds of reels of thread, needles and palms for the sailmakers, barrels of pitch, vats of varnish, mile upon mile of different weights of cordage. There were, however, no beasts of burden to carry these supplies from ship to shore for here the rules of productivity were perverted and efficiency came second to punishment. Every barrel and sack off the *Prince Leopold* was transported up the slip on a human back wearing the same, hated yellow jacket that James Porter had worn on the chain gang.

When the stores were disembarked, Porter was taken before Captain Briggs. It was not a happy meeting. 'I found him everything but a gentleman,' Porter said. 'A complete tyrant—he ordered what clothes I had on to be burned and gave me a suit of yellow and sent to work.' For Captain Briggs, James Porter was an 'out-and-outer', one of those who 'would strain every point to get away', and he must be treated with unremitting severity.

The little society that Captain Briggs controlled at Macquarie Harbour was a microcosm of Governor Arthur's island-wide vision of perfectly oiled penal cogs and godly screws: a snakes-and-ladders board of punishment and reward. The top tier of Harbour convicts consisted of tradesmen: gardeners, blacksmiths, carpenters, cooks and the sawyers who worked in a mist of menthol oil. The hard labour was done by the men in work gangs, differentiated from the top tier and from each other by conditions of work and petty privileges of diet and accommodation. Timber was felled and sawed by the senior outgangs, trustworthy enough to be issued with sharp tools from the engineering store and to live in camps on the mainland. Their privilege was permission to go fishing or dig kangaroo pits. Next down, with their eyes on the rung above, were the lesser outgangs, rowed across to the mainland each morning and brought back to huts on Sarah Island each night. These men built the log-roads down which the felled timber was rolled through the forest to the water's edge, then chained the trunks together on the beach to form vast rafts and towed them across to Sarah. There, the worst of all tasks was done by the 'home-gang' at the bottom of the heap: wading chest-deep into the water, those under punishment or suspicion wearing leg-irons that opened their sores to salt, these men dismantled the rafts and hauled the twelve-ton logs up the slip with no other power than that provided by comrades set like beasts to the capstan. Even among the home-gang there was hierarchy. Reoffenders and recent arrivals slept and ate not in the grim village of Sarah, but on tiny Grummet Island, half a mile away, with no privileges at all. This was to be James Porter's life and it was 'nothing but misery flogging and starvation'.

He rose before daybreak each morning for a bowl of the ubiquitous skilly. At dawn, he descended crude stone steps, washed by waves, and climbed aboard one of a fleet of small boats, two armed soldiers in each, and was rowed across to the docks of Sarah for 12 hours' hard labour, unbroken even for food. He was wet when he embarked, wet for much of the day and wet again when he returned at night. He could not kindle a proper fire, for only green wood was allowed on Grummet and it spat and smoked. He slept each night as part of a steaming, shivering mass in 'a truly Wretched Barracks, in so crowded a state as to be scarcely able to lay down on their sides—to lay upon their backs was out of the Question'. His clothes were never dry, his belly never full and his body never quite free of sores. Here, he and the other men must wait for the commandant's grace to lift them to the next level, house them in the Sarah Island penitentiary huts and perhaps allot them to an outgang or apprenticeship in a workshop.

Porter's new home was a smaller society than Hobart Town, where convicts had mingled with the free; and a more exposed one, for the lower a convict sank, the more he was watched. In the towns, ticket-of-leave convicts on their way up reclaimed individuality by means of trade, possessions, marriage, a stake in the land, the exchange of a number for a name. On the chain gangs, the irons that bound the men together symbolised the fusion of individuals into a nameless unit of labour. By the time convicts descended to Macquarie Harbour, they had become nothing more than a homogenous, many-headed mass of badness. Fewer prisoners, but more guards; greater visibility, less identity: these were two of the penal formulae of Van Diemen's Land and, with this level of surveillance, Commandant Briggs wrote of his confidence that the men had 'given up all idea of absconding'. He was wrong. Even on the islands of Macquarie Harbour, there were those who logged the movement of guards and guard boats, and hoped and plotted. They built bark coracles and hid them in caves; they made crude weapons from bits of filched iron and heavy wood and kept them lashed to their bodies or buried where informers would not find them.

Macquarie Harbour reflected Governor Arthur's regime not only in its rigid differentiation of penal rank but also in its security, for if the island as a whole leaked like a sieve, the Harbour was its leakiest part. This was the third, unacknowledged penal formula: the harsher the regime, the greater the prisoners' desire to escape it.

During its first six years of existence, one in eight convicts had fled the Harbour, heading for the bushrangers' gangs or the farms of the east—perhaps because, during the same period, one in seven had been flogged for 'rebelliousness', 'insolence' and 'refusal to work'. Captain Briggs, despite Porter's comment on him, was a better man than his predecessors and by the time Porter arrived, he had made the Harbour a slightly better place. Nevertheless, with most of its inmates brutalised and despairing, pursuit of bolters continued to be a frequent excitement. One officer was permanently on lookout duty on the hill behind the Sarah Island penitentiary, scanning the outgangs in Phillip Island, the River Gordon and the gardens on the mainland for smoke, the soldiers' signal that someone had gone. A buzz would go round the work-gangs; some would wish the bolter silent luck, others cared for no one's luck but their own and some had lost interest even in that. Then messages were flagged to a quivering Mr Lucas at the Gates in case the fugitive was attempting escape by boat and the dogs were unleashed and set on his trail in case he had headed for the hills. It was rare for a bolter to outrun the dogs and the trackers. If he did, it was rarer still for him to survive the bush. Those caught were brought back to be tied to the triangle and flogged until they were unconscious or the surgeon declared their lives in danger. The rest died, snake-bitten, starved, frozen or speared by the Aborigines who lived unseen and resentful on the north-west coast. Only eight of perhaps 150 bolters were ever reported to have 'reached the cultivated area of the island'. A couple had become legends.

A bold Lancastrian forger called Matthew Brady had attempted to stow away on an England-bound vessel and had been sent to the Harbour in its early days. There, he was put to work on the mainland potato plots. One day in 1824, when the commandant came from Sarah Island to inspect his work, Brady and 13 mates seized the whaleboat that had brought him, rushed the Gates with Mr Lucas just behind and sailed for Hobart, pursued all the way. Brady briefly ruled the hinterland of Hobart and became that most charismatic of figures, the chivalrous bandit: handsome above the kerchief which partly covered his face, protective of the female, the young, the old and the wronged, reputed to steal only from those who deserved it. So popular did he become that when Governor Arthur posted rewards for his capture—*it has caused Governor Arthur much concern that a person known as Matthew Brady is at large . . .* —the only reply received was an impertinent one from the man himself—*it has caused Matthew Brady much concern that a person known as Governor Arthur is at large. Twenty gallons of rum will be given to any person that can deliver his person to me . . .* Matt Brady had been arrested after a dazzling two years in the bush, and was executed before weeping crowds in April 1826.

Only one other Harbour bolter reached Hobart. Alexander Pierce had also seized a whaleboat but had gone east, not west, ditching it at the head of the Gordon River and making off on foot. Seven men had gone with him. They were among the first white men ever to see the primeval forest of western Tasmania, country which hardy bushwalkers still leave alone. After a week of rain, hunger and the most laborious of progress, they killed the weakest and ate him. Four days later, still climbing the unending gullies, they killed and ate the second. When Alexander Pierce was found by an east-coast farmer five weeks later, he was the only one of the gang still alive. He confessed to murder and cannibalism but the authorities did not believe him, thinking these tales only the product of a depraved convict mind. They sent him back to the Harbour, where he absconded again with another desperate man. This time, he was taken two days out by the dogs, with a lump of human meat in his pocket. His companion, dead and disfigured, was found a little way off.

The feats of brave Macquarie bolters were already part of convict folklore when James Porter arrived at the Harbour, and the stories had spread across the island by song and tall tale. What was not material for campfire entertainment were the darker stories of the Macquarie men who did not fight, nor escape, nor even resist but simply gave up hope. There were many of them, for although Macquarie Harbour was in part a place of rebellion, it was in greater part a place of despair. Those sent for trial in Hobart 'declared', said Lieutenant-Governor Sorell proudly, 'that they would rather suffer death than be sent back', adding, 'it is the feeling which I am most anxious to be kept alive'. During his year on Grummet Island, James Porter saw murders 'frequently committed—twice or three times a month with a view to ridding themselves of a wretched existence. Out of every 100 young men 96 would have sore backs—in fact so bad was the treatment that death was preferable'. On Sarah, one man sank his axe into the head of another walking in front of him one day because, he explained, there was no tobacco in the Harbour and he would rather be hanged than go without. Another killed a comrade because he was 'tired of his life'. Those capitally convicted in the Harbour thanked the hangman and only smiled at the chaplain when he begged them to repent and save their souls; another observer noted an 'apathy of conscience quite incorrigible' in men who had lost faith in a humanity that could condemn them to this existence, and no hope of a better one.

In 1832, two years after Porter's arrival, a pair of brave Quaker missionaries named Backhouse and Walker visited the Harbour. They went among the men, listened and were shocked by their attitude to the grace of the Lord. For these devout men, despair—the absence of hope—was the greatest sin against God, yet 'several', wrote James Backhouse, 'had the notion that all who came to Macquarie Harbour were predestined to hell'. These were the men whom overseers or more powerful hut-mates had picked on for years for rape or servitude or some other type of tyranny, for whom the end of their Harbour sentence had faded to invisibility beyond too many days of degradation. For those who could see beyond the Harbour and imagine a return to the world, what awaited? Many still had years of their original sentence left to run; those who, like James Porter, had been sentenced to transportation for the term of their natural life could expect nothing after Macquarie Harbour but a return to the conditions in which they had committed the crime for which they had been sent here. Release, reoffence, another sentence: the sad, eternal facts of prison life would dictate the future of most Macquarie men.

Newly strolling among the convicts when Porter appeared was a Methodist minister, the Reverend William Schofield. For its first ten years, the Harbour did not have a clergyman. It was an indication of how irredeemable those here were thought to be, not only by themselves, but by the authorities who thought the sacraments wasted upon such creatures. The first Harbour missionary had found the commandant living in sin and immediately turned round and headed back to Hobart. William Schofield, who had volunteered for the post, was more concerned with the convicts than their masters. He represented the other side of the penal coin: while the officers worked for the punishment of criminals, he worked for the reclamation of sinners. Holding Sunday services in the shipwright's shed, for there was no church, he squinted in the light of a skylight let into the ceiling for him to read from his Bible to a congregation shuffling on its feet before him, for there were no seats. Governor Arthur had approved Schofield's presence at the Harbour, although his thinking was different from the reverend's own. Arthur believed religious instruction necessary not to redeem sinners but so 'they should be more sensitive to the degradation of their punishment and that severity should not be thrown away upon callous indifference'.

The governor might have disdained pastoral care but Reverend Schofield was a gentler man, concerned to save the souls trapped in the miserable bodies around him. Like his Quaker brethren, he believed that it was by despair that 'Satan had long kept some of them in bondage, and still kept others from seeking deliverance from sin, under the persuasion that it was of no use for them to try to turn to righteousness.' At Schofield's instigation, religious meetings and then a 'night school' were established on Sarah Island, with teachers chosen from the better-behaved and literate prisoners to instruct their comrades in reading, writing and arithmetic. It was 'well attended', wrote another officer, 'and many of the scholars derived the double advantage of receiving instruction, and at the same time, passing their leisure hours away from the society of their more vicious companions'.

Some convicts were grateful for the reverend's night school, for not all saw bolting as the best means of escape from wretchedness. A few did find solace in the spiritual exercise encouraged by the Reverend Schofield at his 'conversational meetings' and entered a world of repentance and contemplation, 'lay[ing] hold of the offers of mercy through a crucified redeemer'. Not all, however, chose the way of the Lord. Some found a secular route, keeping their heads down, refusing to be antagonised, logging good behaviour, counting the days until the end of this sentence, then the days until the end of the next one, hanging on for a ticket of leave. A few escaped servitude by gaining the rank of overseer, exchanging the comradeship of labour for lonely authority, petty privileges and the resentment of those they had left behind. Luckier others, better regarded by ranks above and below them, escaped the brutal labour of the logging gangs through apprenticeships in the yards, protected by separate accommodation from the violence of the desperate, spoken to in words that were not only insult and order, working in yards that smelt of civilisation: leather, turpentine, paint and tar.

Still there were some whose thoughts of escape were couched in the simple terms of bolting and James Porter was one of these. Neither James Backhouse nor William Schofield are mentioned in his memoir of Macquarie life, for he was not interested in what they offered. Just over a year after Porter's arrival, he was promoted from Grummet to Sarah Island. Once again, however, the system of reward and deterrent failed to inspire him. Shortly afterwards, he was sentenced to three weeks on bread and water for 'leaving his work contrary to orders'. Nine days were remitted from this relatively mild punishment but, becoming more determined as he had after too many reprimands in Hobart Town, five weeks later he spotted 'a slight chance for liberty' and bolted again.

'The case,' he would write, 'was this. Twenty of us were going over on the main to Kelly's Bason [sic] to get some logs on the pits for sawyers.' Kelly's Basin was an inlet on the north shore of the mainland, near the head of the estuary, home to an outgang of sawyers and lime-burners. It was from here that Alexander Pierce had begun his grotesque excursions and many others had escaped to die in the bush. Fully aware of the dangers, Porter was nonetheless 'determined to gain my point or perish in the attempt'. As their boat touched land, James Porter and two others leapt out with their axes raised, surprising the guard, threw tools and oars overboard to 'deprive anyone who may have felt inclined to resist us', pushed the vessel as far out as they could and disappeared.

It was not Porter's plan to make west or north overland along the routes where so many had already perished. He and his mates had their eye on the Gordon River, for they believed, wrongly, that if they could reach its source, they 'would soon reach Head Quarters [Hobart Town]'. From Hobart, the game of making Bruny and the oil ships would start all over again. Nor did they mean to struggle along the river banks, for they knew that impassable scrub grew right down to the water there. They would make upriver by boat, and they knew where one of these was to be had.

All day, they lay concealed on the summit of a hill near Kelly's Basin, watching as the Sarah Island guard came out to the assistance of the whaleboat drifting in the river. Under cover of night, they descended and swam across to the camp of an outgang opposite Phillip Island, where they crept among the tents and stole as much food as they could carry. Leaving their loot on the beach, they then swam out to the island, knowing the gardening gang stationed there kept an illicit canoe for fishing, woke one of the men and forced him to hand it over. The second day was dangerous, spent hiding in foliage at the water's edge. At daybreak, a launch was sent from Sarah

Island to bring in all the outgangs, lest they should be tempted to help or join the runaways. The theft of food was discovered and five soldiers were left where the plundered gang had been, with 'orders to shoot us if they could come near us'. At dark, the three men came out of the long grass, pushed off and slipped away in the canoe.

If the theft of the Phillip Island canoe went unreported, then the trackers would be concentrating their efforts in the bush; and the Phillip Island convicts would not report the theft, for then they must also confess to having owned an illegal craft and be flogged. This was the hope that sustained the three escapees on their first full day of paddling from bend to bend of the Gordon River, watching for signs of any of the felling gangs that worked at intervals along the waterway. They slept tucked away in a creek some miles from the head of the river and pushed off again at dawn, encouraged by the lack of pursuit. As they were working their way around the shore of a deep bay to avoid the river currents, a logging launch rowed by two dozen men rounded the point, saw them, and gave chase. There was no possibility of losing their pursuers by water; the runaways headed for shore, abandoned the canoe with all their supplies and ran for cover.

What came next was horribly reminiscent of Porter's dash through the bush to Oyster Cove. The three men found themselves ensnared, 'plunging, hacking, stumbling, snatching at branches to save a fall, [bringing] down a shower of wet at every touch', soaked to the skin and very soon exhausted. They had little idea of direction. They spent that night 'in the wet laying close to each other for warmth'. The trackers found them next morning and the soldiers panting up behind fired muskets over their heads to wake them. 'We could not walk,' Porter recalled, 'they had to get us to the boat by carrying us and in this wretched state we were brought back to the Settlement and in this state we were ordered by the Commandant to a dark cell in the Gaol.'

For the crime of 'absconding into the woods', James Porter was sentenced to 100 lashes, six months in irons and two months' imprisonment in gaol at night.

3

The Boat Crew

James Porter's escape up the River Gordon never stood a chance of success. It had been clear for some time that bolting landwards, into the island, was useless. Beyond the almost impassable bush, settlement was invading the interior, with magistrates and constables behind. Worse, since 1828, Governor Arthur had declared martial law in the central region in an effort to drive the Aborigines out into the corners of the island. More soldiers and more policemen had been brought in to enforce the law and subsequently Van Diemen's Land was not the bushranger's playground it had been when Matthew Brady made his name. Bolters from the Harbour could now only look west, towards the ocean, and this was even more daunting than the gullies and mountains of the east. For a seaward escape, they must steal some boat in which to rush the Gates; then navigate, with a minimum of instruments, some of the least-known of the world's waters and finally make some destination civilised enough to offer a decent life, yet sufficiently obscure that the forces of Britain would not know where to look for them.

Such a combination of luck and skill seemed impossible. Still there was one man in Macquarie Harbour who had first-hand tales of just

such adventure. He was convict William Swallow, seaman collier on
Tyneside in a long-ago life, now a legendary colonial character who
had accumulated more failed escapes and secondary sentences than
any other old Harbour lag. As a lifer in New South Wales twenty
years ago, Swallow had stolen a schooner in Sydney Cove and been
sent to Van Diemen's Land for the attempt. Escaping from the ship
that was taking him to Hobart, he made it to Rio de Janeiro but
remorseless British authorities got him back. Sent to Macquarie
Harbour in 1828 aboard the government brig *Cyprus* with thirty
other convicts, he hijacked that vessel, put the officers on shore with
a miserable quantity of food and no boat and made for Canton. There
he passed himself off as Captain Waldron of the wrecked ship
Edward, a story that held for a while, but only a while. In 1830, he
was back in a London courtroom, informed on, 'in expectation of
the reward for an escaped convict' by the man whom his wife had
bigamously married when he was sent to Australia. In August 1831,
Swallow was joined in Macquarie Harbour by two more of the
Cyprus gang, recognised and recaptured by British officers in the
South Pacific.

Even those few who escaped the island could not, it seemed, evade
the roaming clutch of the British navy and in a prison routine
enforced by an experienced commandant and guards, opportunity
for repeating such an escape was, in any case, vanishingly slim. The
settlement was full of small boats, watched constantly by convict
and soldier alike. With ten years' experience of bolters, every official
of every rank followed procedures to keep them out of the prisoners'
hands. Each of the whaleboats which carried the men to and from
work had an armed soldier in the bow. Anywhere that visitors
landed—on the smaller islands, or outlying camps—their boat was
immediately pushed several lengths back into the water to await
them. Discovery of any homemade craft, even the flimsiest coracle

of stretched skin and bark, brought a flogging. The wood sent to Grummet Island for the men's fires was examined before it went to make sure none of it would float. A strict guard was kept on the logs hauled up the Sarah Island slips by the home-gangs, for these had been used as the most primitive of rafts, straddled and hand-paddled hopelessly into capture. Yet sooner or later all repressive regimes must slip up, mistakes are made, guards grow tired or bored, or drink, or run into debt or fall in love and some of the Macquarie men were preparing for just such a moment.

Not long after James Porter's arrival in the Harbour, a remarkable man had come to assist Mr Hoy, Master Shipwright at the Harbour. He was the Lancastrian convict gunsmith John Barker. Barker had been in Van Diemen's Land less than two years and had already incurred ten days on the treadwheel, a second term of fourteen years' transportation for receiving, time on the chain gang and a final sentence of transportation for life for attempting escape from that grim place. On top of this accumulation of Vandemonian sentences, John Barker had served four earlier years in another penal settlement at Bermuda. Nevertheless, he was a skilled man in an island woefully short of skills and this had outweighed his atrocious record. One large new brig was on the Sarah Island stocks, construction of her hull only just underway, and Mr Hoy, privy to plans for Macquarie Harbour's future, knew her launch date was unfeasibly optimistic without the help of tradesmen like Barker. John Barker had therefore been sent to work as overseer of the Sarah Island forge, a privileged position that brought with it respect, superior accommodation and even his own assigned servant. He worked well, carrying out Mr Hoy's directions to the letter, mending the soldiers' firearms and instructing his apprentices.

What John Barker's superiors did not know was that he was also taking tuition himself, quietly and in private. His tutor was an educated convict, one William Phillips who had, before his crime and conviction, worked for the East India Company, the enormous trading concern that ran British interests in India. William Phillips had knowledge of great value to those who turned their eyes towards the ocean. As part of his East India Company work, he had learnt 'deduced reckoning', the ancient technique of navigation used before a method of calculating longitude had been discovered and disseminated. This knowledge he was now sharing with the quiet John Barker, who drew none but admiring attention to himself and had sufficient patronage in the matter of placing men in comfortable jobs to make his lessons worth Mr Phillips' while.

Those who still dreamt of escape from Macquarie Harbour did not know that changes in the island map were underway which would offer them opportunity, if they were brave and quick enough to take it. Six months before James Porter was sentenced to hard labour in the Harbour for his breakaway to Bruny Island, a Lieutenant-Colonel Logan had been sent to inspect the Tasman Peninsula, an isolated promontory sixty miles south of Hobart Town. Here, 150 twice-convicted prisoners lived with fifteen soldiers under the command of Dr Russell, a military surgeon bewildered by this addition to his colonial duties. He struck the irons from prisoners in his care and begged Hobart for better clothes, better food and better materials for their huts. Governor Arthur, obsessed with penning up the island's Aborigines, had as yet little time to spare for this outpost but a new gaol-within-a-gaol was gradually growing there. By the end of 1832, Lieutenant-Colonel Logan was sure that only a fast patrol boat to search the coast for escapees was required before the new labour camp on the south coast could replace the old one on the west.

Macquarie Harbour was expensive to run and its costs had never been covered by the production of its ship and timber yards. Its existence was justified not by profit but by its isolated location and this was about to be compromised. The Van Diemen's Land Company, established by private investors to develop land and lease it to settlers, had recently made exploratory expeditions to the northwest of the island and had established a base at Circular Head, only 80 miles north of the Harbour. Opening up the lonely west coast to grazing would bring prosperity. It would further harry the hated blacks. It would bring in more amenable yeoman farmers and create more opportunities for the remaking of men gone wrong but it would cost Macquarie Harbour its greatest asset—isolation.

In August 1831, Commandant Captain Briggs asked to be relieved of his post at the Harbour and in his stead came Major James Baylee. Major Baylee was rare among those given their own little fiefdom of penal authority: he was a decent man and his influence changed the harsh tenor of Harbour life. He took command of only 150 prisoners, for a steady trickle of the more submissive had been transferred to Port Arthur over the last several months, each supply brig from Hobart taking a few more off as she left. The men who remained in the Harbour were those who had either clocked up the most floggings, the most chains and the longest periods of confinement or those who possessed indispensable skills for the continuing work in the shipyard and on the boats.

Among those who came most quickly to the new commandant's notice was James Porter, under sentence of flogging and heavy labour in irons for his attempted escape up the Gordon River. Once more, Porter would later recall, he was saved from his punishment by intercession: the Major had not been long enough an officer in a penal settlement to watch with equanimity as men were half-killed at the triangle. The sentence was reduced. No wonder Porter remembered the man fondly: 'no more sad countenances,' he said, 'when Major Bailey [sic] took charge; all was joy beaming in every countenance'. It was Baylee who took Porter out of the logging gangs and sent him to the pilot's establishment at the South Head. Not only would this remove him from the temptations of Kelly's Basin and the Gordon River but there were recent vacancies for seamen-convicts at the mouth of the estuary.

Although an oar in the pilot launch was in many ways a preferable billet to the cells of Grummet or the Sarah penitentiary, manning the boat was dangerous work. It was 'surprising', wrote a landsman at the Sarah Island commissariat, 'to observe through what terrific seas the pilot would take his boat out to the ships making the harbour'. The same government brig that had recently brought Major Baylee to the Harbour had, two years previously, witnessed the complete destruction of Mr Lucas's launch. The brig's captain, keeping a prudent ten-mile offing from the shore, had seen the pilot launch emerge from the Gates despite a gathering south-westerly gale to be swamped by the waves halfway to the vessel she was attempting to guide in. All hands were lost. The next Harbour pilot, George Bowhill, was no less courageous than his predecessor. One day in August, when Major Baylee had been in charge for four months and the gales were again at their howling winter worst, the flag went up on De Witts hill. A whaleboat was at the bar. The pilot boat went out, manoeuvred so skilfully close that, even in the wild waves, Mr Bowhill could leap aboard, then pulled away to wait where the water was gentler. However, even Mr Bowhill's experience was insufficient that day: the whaleboat capsized as she crossed the bar and all aboard were drowned. The pilot's was among the 20 bodies dragged across the scouring sand and out to sea and James Porter was sent up from Sarah Island to take over a dead man's seat in the launch. Appointed coxswain, he was given a bunk in the boat-crew's hut on the South Head.

Two of the men who had already slung their hammocks here had familiar faces, though older and harder than when he had last seen them in Hobart Town. Both had been fellow seamen aboard the *Prince Leopold*. With Police Number 299, Porter's acquaintance went even further back. Charles Lyon, a 28-year-old Scot, had disembarked the *Asia* convict-ship 25 men ahead of James Porter in 1824 and the two men had similar backgrounds. Lyon, too, had gone to sea at an early age, aboard an uncle's smack in the River Tay on the east coast of Scotland. His early sailing career had been brief as he had been sentenced for breaking and entering a house in Perth when only 18 years old. Sentenced to 14 years but with youth on his side and his hulk record 'orderly', Lyon had restrained himself in his first years on the island and respected the system. Within two years of his arrival, he had committed only one misdemeanour: 'indecent and disorderly conduct in company with Ann Ryan in the Bush', for which he was given 50 lashes. When the two men had last met aboard the *Prince Leopold*, Charles Lyon had seemed to be on his way up the ladder while James Porter was making his wilful way down. Since then, however, Lyon had followed the trajectory of so many long-term convicts. In 1829, absence from the vessel saw him demoted to the barracks and fighting in the barracks saw him on the treadwheel. In 1830, for repeated insolence, drunkenness, breaking from barracks and neglect of duty he was sent to a chain gang, attempted to bolt and was captured. By 1831, he had turned vicious. Indecent conduct degenerated into the rape for which his sentence was increased to transportation for life and he was sent to the Harbour. Here he was bo'sun on the pilot boat and a sullen figure.

James Lesley, the other man from the *Prince Leopold*, was another graduate of the barracks, the treadwheel, the triangle and the chain gang, in Macquarie Harbour since 1830. Described in official records as a 'shipwright' from Bristol, he can have done no more than start an apprenticeship in the shipyards there, for James Lesley had taken to crime from an early age. Sentenced to death at Monmouth for 'stealing within a dwelling house', he was pardoned, probably on account of his youth. Soon after he was twice accused of housebreaking. Twice acquitted because of lack of evidence, his record nevertheless told against him when he was found guilty in 1825 of mugging a lady in a Bristol park and stealing her purse. He was sentenced to transportation for life and was in trouble within months of his arrival in Van Diemen's Land. Heavy punishment had not cured him of repeated neglect of duty, pilfering of government supplies, absences without leave, drunkenness, breaking curfew and 'falsely representing himself as a free man' and so James Lesley, too, was now heaving an oar in the Macquarie Harbour pilot boat.

Despite its dangers, working for the pilot offered a better existence than the logging gangs for Lyon, Lesley, Porter and the other nine or so men employed there. It was a smaller community than Grummet or Sarah Island, and, with a guard of six soldiers—one for every two convicts—had an even higher level of surveillance. Nevertheless, success here depended on skill, not just on obedience and mute, brute labour. There was respect as well as discipline. The soldiers lived somewhat apart from the convicts, passing the time with cards and rum until relief came from Sarah, interfering little in the work of the pilot. The convict crew lived in huts closer to the water's edge, near the pilot's own 'comfortable cottage', next to which were 'good out-houses, a good garden and potato field'. When there was no work in the boat to be done, the men of the crew were employed here, tilling and digging, fertilising with weed gathered from along the long, sandy beach of the South Head.

The Heads also offered a greater variety of amusement than the islands. There were the beaches to be scoured after strong winds for shells, sponges, the flotsam of old wreckage and sometimes the bodies of blackfish, 'a small species of whale', left stranded upon the shore. There were the elusive 'natives' to spy on when they appeared on the North Head, across the water, and sometimes even crossed the river to the Europeans' camp. They came 'occasionally, and only in small groups', aboard precarious floats made of tea-tree bark lashed with grass, and were 'said to be shy, but not to have committed any outrage'—or so believed Quaker James Backhouse, passing on this received opinion without question along with the report that 'one of them exchanged a girl of about fourteen years of age for a dog, with the people at the Pilot Station but the girl not liking her situation was taken back, and the dog returned'. Only for the superstitious— and seamen, despite their scars and tattoos and daredevilry in the rigging, were a notoriously superstitious lot—was this a less cushy berth. The Gates, the deceptive beach and the spit over which they looked had seen many wrecks. Bodies of men involved in escape or accident had frequently rolled ashore here 'dreadfully disfigured by the fish' and their ghosts were said to haunt the estuary. Those on flagstaff duty behind the huts did not know whether the shapes they saw at dawn and dusk were drowned men returned, natives uprisen and coming to get them with spears or just movements of the mist.

The pilot sent from Hobart to replace the drowned Mr Bowhill was a Scottish seaman, Captain Charles Taw. With him came an assigned servant, James Macfarlane. Taw was not a natural master of convicts, lacking both the bonhomie that allowed Major Baylee to walk safely among the gangs without a bodyguard; and the severity of Mr Lucas, who had been 'a man with whom the Prisoners can take no liberty either in his Boat or a Shore' and who 'kept the Prisoners at such a distance that they Seldom approach his Station'. Taw's weakness for strong liquor was soon notorious and cannot have been helped by the loneliness of his new post, where company was a choice between the soldiers who would take his rum but offer no friendship to a superior rank, and the convicts whom he must command the next morning.

With Captain Taw came confirmation of the rumours that had circled among the prisoners since the departure of Commandant Briggs, whispered, denied, misbelieved, whispered again. The Harbour was to be evacuated and abandoned. The boat currently under construction, newly named the *Frederick* for one of Governor Arthur's sons, was to be the last Harbour-built vessel: Captain Taw was here not just to carry out the duties of the pilot but also to bring her to Hobart. The news raised hopes among those men who thought that anywhere must be better than the Harbour, but for Mr Hoy it brought fresh difficulties. With Port Arthur draining his workforce, Mr Hoy needed to get his unfinished brig off the stocks and launched but work was not progressing as fast as hoped and he had fallen ill, and could not shake the illness off.

That winter, as the exodus from Macquarie Harbour to Port Arthur continued, two more skilled convicts were sent the other way. John Fare and John Jones were not normal Harbour material as Governor Arthur's later report on them does not mention any colonial crimes; indeed, arriving in Van Diemen's Land in July and already in the Harbour by August, they had had no time to commit any misdeeds. Nor were they repeat offenders. Although Jones, like John Barker, had been transported to Bermuda for an earlier crime, the Hulk Reports (official reports on a convict's behaviour while waiting to embark transport ships in England) for both men described them as 'orderly' and their Surgeon's Reports marked them as 'good'. The fact was that both were accomplished professional seamen. Before his conviction for housebreaking in Southampton, 27-year-old Fare, another Scot, had been 'captain of the fo'c'sle' on a 74-gun frigate. This, although not an official rank, was the working designation of the most experienced seaman before the mast of a large ship, to whom the other men looked to fill in the detail of the officers' orders. Less is known of the seafaring experience of the

Liverpudlian who came to the Harbour with him, 41-year-old John Jones, except that he gave his trade as 'seaman' on arrival in Hobart (confirmed by tattoos of mermaids and compasses) and he had been caught in a small boat off Ratcliffe Pier in London with the proceeds of two separate hauls from a night's ship-raiding in September 1832— clothes and watches stealthily lifted from the state cabins where the ships' masters were sleeping. His seamanship was deemed satisfactory by the officials who examined him in Hobart and both men were sent up specifically to help handle the brig on what all now acknowledged would be a very late maiden voyage. In Mr Hoy's opinion, she would not be ready for launch until mid-January.

On Sarah Island, the fragrant goods of the commissariat were packed up, labelled and sent south. Gradually, the guard was reduced. Grummet Island was abandoned and the number of men in the logging gangs diminished with each boat that left for Hobart Town or Port Arthur. In October, the Harbour was given a month in which to pack itself up. There was a hitch, however: the *Frederick*, as Mr Hoy had warned, was not going to be ready when the final evacuation came. Governor Arthur sent orders that it was to be dismantled and the timber sent to Port Arthur but Major Baylee replied that work was too far advanced for this to be practicable.

It was therefore decided that a party of carpenters and seamen, with four soldiers to guard them, would be left behind to finish the *Frederick* and sail her to Port Arthur under Captain Taw's command. Mr James Tate, a free man living at the Harbour, would act as his first mate but the others would be convicts. It was up to Major Baylee to decide who these men would be but he seems to have deputed this task to Captain Taw, presuming that the captain would make a better assessment of skill than he.

No one knows when Captain Taw made his choice or on what grounds, exactly. Perhaps he considered the chosen men indispensable for their skills; perhaps they happened to be the men in sight when he had to write names on a list. Some were obvious choices. John Fare and John Jones had already been assigned this duty in Hobart. They could not manage without John Barker at the forge. Taw's own assigned servant, James Macfarlane, must stay to cook his meals and do his laundry and Mr Hoy's convict servant, William Nicholls, would stay to do the same for him. The other choices were a little more arbitrary.

Three were ships' carpenters from the Sarah yards whose recent records were clean. John Dady, yet another Scot, had been transported for life for picking a handkerchief worth seven shillings from a pocket in Fleet Street when only 16. He gave his trade then as 'brick-layer' but had since, after a long period of rebellion, become a skilled carpenter and had committed no recent offences. There was long-term Harbour resident Billy Shires, a Yorkshireman sentenced to a life term in 1820 for highway robbery (mugging), in the Harbour since 1831 for an unspecified felony and the second oldest of the group at 38. He, too, had stayed out of trouble since his arrival in the Harbour. The third carpenter was Benjamin Russen, aged 28, much scarred and tattooed. He had been a weaver when he was taken from the Norfolk Assizes in 1822 and transported for life. In Hobart, he had been assigned to a boatbuilder or chandler, from whom he promptly stole '2 lbs boat nails the property of his master' and repeatedly ran away. He had only been on the island a year when three offences saw him transported on the first boats to Macquarie Harbour. Russen had managed to learn enough boat work to eventually lift himself out of the logging gangs, despite several early escape attempts and repeated disobedience. His record, too, had been clean since January 1829.

The last of the carpenters was chosen because he was John Barker's assigned servant rather than for his skills: he was still an apprentice, and a rather pathetic figure. At four foot eleven, William Cheshire was the result of generations of malnourishment in his 'native place' of Birmingham, from where he had been transported for life at the age of 17, convicted of burglary. After a pathetic history of misdemeanour while an assigned servant to a country master— 'disobedience', 'household insolence', 'household drunkenness', for which his runty frame was stretched to the triangle, sent to the treadwheel and fed, in isolation, on bread and water—Cheshire had ended up in Macquarie Harbour. Here he had been relatively fortunate, being taken under Mr Hoy's, and then John Barker's, wing.

When he came to select the seamen who would assist him in piloting the brig to Hobart, it was natural that Captain Taw should look to his own boat-crew. Charles Lyon, Scottish fisherman and bo'sun, and James Porter, London deckhand and coxswain, were chosen. With them came James Lesley, Bristol mariner, convict oarsman and Porter's *Prince Leopold* shipmate.

'I regarded them as "recommended men",' he would protest later, attempting vainly to defend this preposterous selection of brutes and bolters to an incandescently angry Arthur.

Between them (and their records are incomplete), they had clocked up 800 lashes, eight secondary sentences of transportation, eight periods on the chain gang, 67 days on the treadwheel, two previous sentences of transportation to Bermuda, one previous capital conviction, a rape, three assaults, eight burglaries and nine attempts to escape the island.

4

Leaving the Island of Misery

On 25 November 1833, the last 150 men bound for Port Arthur went aboard the government vessels. Major Baylee, camp commandant, took his leave of those who were to remain behind. To the soldiers, he counselled prudence. They were 'to keep watch 2 and 2, the same as a seaman's watch, but not to carry their arms, as there was no necessity for it' but 'to keep an eye on the seamen, to prevent any confusion, and to have their arms in readiness in their berths'. To Mr Hoy, he wished a speedy recovery and entrusted responsibility for the *Frederick* until she was launched. To Captain Taw—perhaps with a quiet word on the dangers of drink to a lonely man—he gave orders to put the convicts on marine rations, including the marine's gill of rum per day (or so, at least, the men were given to understand) and assume command of the *Frederick* from the day of her launch. To the convicts themselves, he gave advice: work well and obey orders, and he would intercede for a ticket of leave for all of them in Hobart Town. 'I felt as much parting with him as from a parent,' said James Porter, 'and I cannot help saying "God prosper him wherever he is."' Then the good major's jolly-boat took him into the river and the small convoy under his command began its last journey from the Harbour. A pile of dry stores, an uncompleted brig, a goat, some swine, a ship's cat, a few potatoes, ten convicts, five free men and four soldiers were left in the deserted estuary.

For three weeks, those remaining worked to finish off the vessel on the stocks, painting, caulking and waterproofing her hull. Oakum (frayed rope), mixed with various fibrous substances—leaves, thick grass—was worked into the seams between the timbers. Above it went layer upon layer of thick, filthy pitch. The carpenters were at work fitting out her interior, putting in the berths and galley. The rudder was hung and the heavy ropes that controlled it were rigged to the helm. A spare set of rough-weather canvas was cut for her two masts, stitched and laced to boom and yards to check its fit, then rolled in sailcloth and bundled into forward lockers. Sails were cut for her tenders, the seven-ton longboat and smaller whaleboat that she would carry aboard. Mr Hoy directed operations when he could but his illness did not allow him to spend full days on the slip. Nor was Captain Taw always present, for he still lived at the pilot's establishment near the Heads, from where he came upriver to check on progress when he was not too drunk. The captain had not given the convicts the daily gill of rum they believed Major Baylee had authorised for them and there was rancorous feeling about this. There was also friction among the prisoners. Some thought they were working harder than others; some were polite to the shipwright and the captain and annoyed when others were not. Charles Lyon did not seem able to behave himself. He disobeyed orders, made threats and 'behav[ed] insolently to the captain'.

William Cheshire caused difficulties of a different sort, for he was one of the despised race of prisoners who ensured their protection not by gaining the respect or fear of peers but by sticking close to the officers. Running little extra errands, he extracted a promise from Mr Hoy that he would add his own good word to that offered by

Major Baylee for 'some indulgence'. He did not ask Mr Hoy's intercession for anyone else.

Whose head was first visited by dreams of hijack? James Porter and Benjamin Russen were both serial bolters. Charles Lyon knew the island's west coastline well after his time as bo'sun of the Harbour pilot's boat and John Fare and John Jones thought themselves capable of managing a small vessel on an ocean passage but it was gunsmith John Barker, universally reckoned 'a most injinious [sic] man at anything', who led the field in skills and confidence. When Captain Taw was drinking, and Mr Hoy sweating in his sickbed, John Barker was at the forge on business of his own, working on the barrels of old soldiers' muskets brought in earlier for repair and hidden when the settlement was evacuated. When these were finished, he began on a set of 'tomahawks', and few men could turn out an axe more efficiently than the overseer of smiths in a logging camp.

No one would later confess to being the first to float the idea of seizing the *Frederick*, but somehow, in these days of minimal surveillance and relaxed routine, nine of the convicts reached agreement. Eight were under sentence of transportation for life, seven since they had stood in court in Britain and the eighth, Charles Lyon, for the rape he had committed in the ninth year of a fourteen-year sentence. Only John Jones was not there for life, and even he had twelve years still to serve before he would be free. Whispers had begun to reach Van Diemen's Land of the first stirrings of the abolitionist movement back home in Britain; of speakers and writers who compared transportation to slavery and called for an end to both—but there had been condemnation of transportation for decades, and yet here they were, in penal servitude in Macquarie Harbour. True, Mr Hoy might put in a good word for them in Hobart Town and so might Major Baylee but they would still be working at His Majesty's pleasure, with the stunted identity of the convict, subject to the malice and disdain of the free. The rumours did not promise enough hope of emancipation that these men would reject the chance of real liberty, so unexpectedly offered, so desperately desired.

Their plan was simple. When launched from Sarah Island, the *Frederick* would have to wait downriver at Wellington Head for a favourable wind and tide to take her across the bar. When this moment came, they would seize her, put the others ashore and head for the ocean. The servants, James Macfarlane, William Nicholls and William Cheshire, were not told of the plan but one day Cheshire, cooking John Barker's meal, heard James Lesley and Benjamin Russen discussing the escape on the far side of the flimsy partition wall in the hut they all shared. Cheshire told Barker what he had heard; Barker reported to the others that his servant knew and Cheshire was taken reluctantly into the secret. They had to hope their opportunity came before one of the fraternity, drunk or afraid or cunning, let slip the plot. Charles Lyon might be a weak link; so might William Cheshire, already suspected of being an officers' nark.

On the day of the *Frederick*'s launch, 16 December, heavy summer rain fell as they greased the skids with tallow. They waited for high tide to bring the water close to where the ship stood on her chocks. When it came, they shot her down the skids into the water, the timber baulks beneath her hull bobbed out and away and she floated. According to Major Baylee's instructions, Captain Taw should have assumed command that day but he was visibly, aggressively drunk, even before the rum saved for the launch party was produced. Mr Hoy had to order the soldiers to take the captain away and confine him until he was sober. They obeyed, restraining the captain in his bunk, and work continued slowly under Mr Hoy's command. Over the following weeks, the men readied the *Frederick* for sail.

Two masts were dragged down the slips, lifted aboard and slotted into their shoes. Yard upon yard of rigging was cut and put in place. Captain Taw continued to drink. When he joined the working parties at Sarah Island one day, he made a bad mess of cutting the lower rigging, but there was no time or not enough materials left in the sheds to cut it anew. Charles Lyon was insolent again; the soldiers took him down to the deserted huts of the pilot's establishment and left him there in solitary confinement. Apart from the wind, the hammer of constant rain on roofs and the few, faint sounds of 19 men and their tools on Sarah Island, the estuary was as silent as it had been when Captain Kelly sailed in 18 years before.

Finally, almost a month after she first hit the water, Mr Hoy passed the *Frederick* as seaworthy, more or less—sufficiently, at least, to take them 300 miles south to Port Arthur. Early on the morning of 12 January 1834, the fast outgoing waters of the Gordon River rushed into the head of the estuary, tugged towards the sea. At ten o'clock, the *Frederick* left Sarah Island on her maiden voyage. No sails could be raised with the winds dead on the nose and the tide behind her. Down went the oarsmen: the only way to give the ship steerage through the water was to send the longboat ahead to tug her laboriously from side to side. At three, with a light south-westerly wind on the beam, they dropped anchor just inside the bar, where Captain Taw hoped to spend the night and be ready for an early start the following day. Close by was the pilot's station, its gardens already reverting to bush. With the reverence for food that characterised any early colonist, and in a moment of sobriety, Captain Taw sent James Porter and William Cheshire to dig up the last of the potatoes and bring them away, with Mr Hoy and two soldiers to guard them. They took everything left in the pilot's stores, fetched Charles Lyon from his confinement, filled water barrels at the stream and rowed them out to the brig.

The potato party had just got back on board when the wind veered to the north-west, raising a heavy surf over the bar. It was too dangerous for the *Frederick* to stay where she was. Hauling up, raising a cautious foresail, Captain Taw took her two miles back up the estuary to anchor in the lee of Wellington Head. At five, 'the sails being furled, and all things made secure', they ate supper. The tide was running fast, now on the flow, and an anchor watch was set. At eight, the rest were in their hammocks. All night, the north-westerly crashed against the far side of Wellington Head and the *Frederick* rocked uneasily in her bay, four soldiers lying sick and damp in steerage, Captain Taw and James Macfarlane in one cabin; poor, ill Mr Hoy attended by William Nicholls in another. While the free men slept, or tried to sleep, ten convicts bunked down in the fo'c'sle at the other end of the ship and discussed their strategy. They would surely have talked over the odds: the wind might change overnight and let them quit the Harbour on the morning tide and head for Port Arthur. This was the place and the moment.

Orders to turn out were shouted forward at break of day, 13 January. Captain Taw and a quartet of oarsmen set out for the bar to swing the lead. They were back by ten. It was impassable. It being clear that the *Frederick* was going nowhere while the north-westerly blew, Captain Taw gave permission to go ashore to anyone who wished to wash his laundry. Every convict brought his clothes up from the fo'c'sle and handed them down in bundles to the men in the whaleboat. Squatting over pools and thrashing linen on rocks, guarded by two bored soldiers eager for Hobart Town, the prisoners held loud and innocent discussions. In the centre of the laundry scrum, John Barker had retrieved the homemade weapons from the bundles of fo'c'sle laundry and was priming the muskets. At half-past four, all were back on board the *Frederick*.

At six, the north-westerly still blew. It was suggested to the soldiers how pleasant it might be for them to go fishing at the point, half-a-mile away, and two of them went to the captain and asked permission. Captain Taw told them they must be back within the hour.

The *Frederick* was quiet as dusk approached: the ten convicts lay chatting in the fo'c'sle; Mr Taw and Mr Hoy were sitting in the aft cabin, drinking rum and waiting for William Nicholls to bring their tea; the other two soldiers and the mate sat and reflected on deck. Some minutes after the fishing party departed, they heard singing from the fo'c'sle below and James Porter's head appeared through the hatch to invite the soldiers to join in. One descended, the other walked forward to the windlass and sat. The song was badly rendered: 'I could not get on,' Porter would recall, 'my mind was in such a state.' It was his task to hold the soldiers' attention while first James Lesley, then William Cheshire and Benjamin Russen, and finally John Fare and John Barker climbed the fo'c'sle ladder, pretending different needs and errands, and got on deck and as far aft as they could. Every man still below, except the soldier guest, was waiting for one sound to interrupt the singing: the stamp of a boot on the boards above to tell them the man on the windlass had been taken.

The signal came. Instantly, Billy Shires was on his feet, a fist raised to the soldier. The man was 'quiet directly'. Charles Lyon and John Jones took and gagged him while Porter and Shires scrambled up on deck. The mate had been taken by Benjamin Russen, who 'came to him with a tomahawk' (one of John Barker's). Shires bundled him down the fo'c'sle scuttle, where two bewildered soldiers were already sitting on a chest, and into the custody of Lyon and Jones. Then he descended into the captain's cabin where Mr Taw and Mr Hoy were tipsy on the rum that should have been sent to the fo'c'sle. From the aft deck, the four bundling up the muskets heard a commotion and pulled the skylight off to see Shires struggling with the men, who were, Porter recalled, 'endeavouring to take his life, they being nearly drunk'. Shires managed to haul himself up through the cabin skylight without injury and knelt with the rest around the open hatch, urging the captain and shipwright 'to come on deck and we would not injure them, but they being groggy refused to do so, defying the whole of us'. It was an uncomfortable stalemate, neither side sure what to do.

For some time, five convicts pointed alarming homemade muskets down the hatch and two staggering, furious men pointed pistols back, roaring defiance and refusal. John Jones, guarding a further malevolent three in the fo'c'sle, listened anxiously for the sound of feet returning to take off the hatch and release him. In the captain's cabin, Mr Taw flourished the bunch of keys that unlocked the arms chest, standing in one corner. Reluctant to provoke a fight, for 'we knew to rush upon drunken men some lives would be lost', but anxious to force surrender before the whaleboat came back or the arms chest was opened, the convicts 'determined to frighten them'. The command was given loudly: 'fire down upon them!' and one of the men's muskets, by accident or luck (skilful aim being out of the question with such crude weapons) went off and the ball knocked the keys from the captain's hand.

'What are you about?' shouted Shires, greatly distressed. 'Are you going to commit murder?'

'No,' the others said.

'It can be done without,' said Shires.

The men below were not so sure. The firing of the muskets, deliberate or not, had 'had the desired effect', and, suddenly sobered, 'they cried out for quarters'.

'Will you deliver yourselves up?' Shires called through the skylight.

'Yes,' said Mr Hoy, 'if you are not disposed to injure us.'

'My life shall be the forfeit if we do. We only want our liberty,' Shires replied and, one by one, the men were pulled through the skylight and had their hands lashed behind them.

Now every member of the crew aboard was secured and the turn had come for those gone fishing in the whaleboat. A musket shot was fired to bring them back on board and the fishing party and its basket of eels came around the point. The moment they were alongside, before the soldiers could realise there were only convicts on deck, James Porter had jumped into the boat, musket cocked, and ordered them to tie up and get out. When these, too, had had their guns taken and their hands secured, they were told they would be put ashore to make their way as best they could to Hobart.

Mr Hoy now 'directed his discourse to John Barker', the man he knew and trusted most, saying '"Who is to be captain of the brig now you have her in your possession?" "I am!"' replied John Barker, "and with the assistance of the men I can navigate her round the world." Mr Hoy then said, "Deluded men, I will now declare before my God, upon the Bible, that upon condition of your giving up the brig, I will not mention it when I reach head-quarters, but will give you all a good character. Barker then made answer "We have the brig in our possession, and we shall keep her; so it is needless for you to mention further about it; for it is liberty we require."'

With one man standing sentinel, Porter, Shires and Barker went down into the cabin with Captain Taw and Mr Hoy, who had asked to take some warm clothing with them. 'We allowed them to take anything they wanted,' said Porter—except the brace of pistols and ammunition Mr Hoy requested 'to protect them from the blacks'. When the others were not looking, Billy Shires wrapped a bottle of spirits in a shirt and gave this and a pocket compass to Mr Hoy, saying 'he was sorry he could not give him any more' and telling him to 'put it up out of sight'. There was blood trickling down Mr Taw's head. The fo'c'sle hatch was finally lifted to reveal a relieved John Jones and his prisoners and one by one the castaways were bid into the jolly-boat and told to pull for the shore, followed by Porter and five others in the whaleboat, 'two of us pulling and four on guard'.

The hijack of the *Frederick* was accomplished. It was a clear, starlit night. On shore, nine resentful men huddled together, reminded every half hour of their lost ship by 'all's well' called by the men on watch across the water, timed by stolen watches.

The ten men aboard the *Frederick* were up at dawn and the subject of sharing supplies was raised. On board, there were three months' provisions: 36 lbs of meat, 50 lbs of biscuit and 12 lbs flour. There were also the potatoes and cabbages dug up the day before from the pilot's garden. In Porter's recollection, it was once again Billy Shires who first insisted on decency. 'Do not [let us] leave them to starve,' he said, 'my proposal is to share the provisions with them as nearly as possible, for there are nine of them and ten of us, and let us trust to Providence; and it will also be the means of preventing them from saying, when they reach head-quarters, that we had used them cruelly, or in a dishonourable manner.' A majority agreed. The precious dry food was split in half and the whaleboat put off with six armed men aboard. Captain Taw set out towards the water's edge but shouts from the whaleboat sent him back. They wished to speak with Mr Hoy, the men said, not the captain. Mr Hoy came, and two soldiers with him, who were told to wade into the water and take off provisions while three mutineers stood guard. As meat, flour, biscuit, iron pots, an axe and a live goat came off, Mr Hoy realised the generosity of the rations being unloaded. The men asked if there was anything further they could bring him from the *Frederick*: 'he wished for some strengthening plaster and bandages from his chest for a pain in the back'. The soldiers added a request for their warm watch coats. When the whaleboat returned to shore, the men brought with them the only two bottles of wine on board, having decided that the ill Mr Hoy had the greater need.

Encouraged by this proof of decency, Mr Hoy made a last appeal, asking the men 'if we would give up the Brig and he would swere on a Bible never to say a word about the matter. We declined any such thing, he said, "Since I find you will not deliver her up, I thank you for your manly conduct throughout and particularly for your kindness to me on account of my illness. I know you have but little provisions to cross the wide ocean and likewise a vessel that is not seaworthy for such a voyage—and may God prosper you in your perilous undertaking." We thanked him and pulled off our hats amid the loud cheers of all on shore wishing us a pleasant voyage'.

'I cannot express my feelings at that moment,' wrote Porter, many years later, 'my heart expanded within me and I believe it was the happiest moment of my life.'

On the morning of 14 January, the mutineers were up at first light to watch for the moment when the tide turned. They needed to catch the high-water slack to move safely down the channel to the Gates, then the fast-flowing ebb which would flush them out across the bar. With the wind funnelling in against them, they, like Captain Taw, were unable to raise sails in order to make their way back downriver to the Heads. Nor could they wait to drift out on the outgoing tide: without the steerage provided by wind in the sails, there would be no way to hold the boat's course through the water and the currents would swirl her about and run her aground on the bar. While the tide was slack, and the currents at rest, they would have to warp out on the kedge, the smaller and more easily portable of the brig's two anchors. The ship's anchor was 'tripped'—lifted until the cable was tight and the anchor's hold on the bottom sufficiently insecure that it could be quickly dislodged. Then one end of a cable was attached to the kedge and the other to the windlass on the *Frederick's* bow, the kedge was taken aboard the whaleboat, rowed some hundred yards ahead and dropped. The men on board raised the ship's anchor and pulled the brig up to the kedge, whereupon the main anchor was dropped and tripped, the kedge raised and rowed further off and the slow, heavy process repeated for two miles, until they came abreast of the Cap and Bonnet islands. There, they hung the whaleboat astern and awaited the turn of the tide.

Those put ashore on the south bank watched as the ship disappeared from view. Their situation was unenviable. It might take a month for the authorities in Hobart Town to wonder why the *Frederick* had not arrived and send out a search party, which itself might take another month to reach them. They would find only corpses, or worse; surely the spectre of the cannibal Pierce entered minds. The nearest Europeans were 80 miles away at Circular Head, the Van Diemen's Land Company station. Given the nature of the ground they would have to cover to get there, they must count on a journey of at least a week. They had no choice. Circular Head was to the north and crossing the estuary here would cut off many hours' painful trekking around the head of the harbour and across the Gordon River. While some had spent the night walking back to the potato gardens to dig up the few poor roots not taken aboard the *Frederick,* others had been at work on a raft, gathering and employing the scant tools and sticks left when the Harbour was evacuated. By morning it was ready, though only slightly more seaworthy than the logs and skin-canoes that had failed to carry so many convicts away from the estuary.

Captain Taw's party, too, had to watch for the high-water slack. Too early, and their little raft would get caught on the incoming tide and be carried back to Sarah Island or beyond; too late and they would be whirled out to sea or smashed against the rocks. Three of the ten climbed aboard and set off for the far bank; seven watched.

Two tiny figures got out on the far side and the raft turned, pushed off and returned. Two more climbed in; again they pushed off. It took four voyages to get all the party to the north bank, soaked, hungry and already tired. There were 80 miles of bush before them. All they could do was begin.

Mid-morning, the tide turned and the slack was gone. The *Frederick* swung slowly about, seven knots' worth of water parting either side of her hull. The anchor was raised for the last time, the whaleboat attached to the windlass and rowed ahead until the cable tightened, the boat's head brought perilously into line with the current. At midday, she shot across the bar but the four men heaving at the whaleboat's oars could not compete with the force of the tide that pushed her bow relentlessly round towards the North Spit. Just the other side of the Gates, she heeled and nearly ran aground, her rudders useless, swung about like a toy on a lake. Yards from the rocks, with John Fare yelling and the men desperately hauling up a gaff-sail on the mizzen, she was saved by a gust of wind that filtered through the reefs from the north-west, its breath caught by the canvas, its power caught by the rudders. They pulled away from the entrance with yards to spare.

Recovering steerage, the *Frederick* stood out to sea, leaving Hell's Gates astern. With only one of her two masts rigged fore-and-aft, she could not sail close into the wind blowing from the south-west, the direction in which they wanted to go. She would have to travel a good distance out into the ocean, then turn and tack back in towards the south-west corner of the island. In these vital first days of flight, any time lost might be fatal. Knowing this and aware there was a seven-ton longboat on deck weighing down the *Frederick*, which could hinder should they need to outrun pursuit, John Barker gave his first orders. The men broke up the whaleboat and threw the pieces overboard, where they were snatched away by one wave and lost to sight beyond the next. They would soon be sodden lumps of driftwood on some miserable beach, and perhaps still are.

> Macquarie Harbour jailers lock the sullen gates no more . . . but lash-strokes sound in every shock of ocean on the dismal rock along that barren shore.
>
> No more the bolters hear the hound that bays upon the wind, and terror-spurred keep onward bound until they drop upon the ground, starved and terror-pinned . . .
>
> But gales that whine among the hills sniff at the savage tracks the hopeless took. The snowfall fills bleak ranges; then the moonlight spills broad arrows on their backs.

The Harbour was abandoned.

5

North Until the
Butter Melts

'As the Roman,' said British Foreign Secretary Viscount Palmerston, 'held himself free from indignity, when he could say "*Civis Romanus sum*" [I am a Roman citizen], so also a British subject, in whatever land he may be, shall feel confident that the watchful eye and the strong arm of England will protect him against injustice and wrong.'

Lord Palmerston came to office in an era when his country's reach was global. The world he surveyed had succumbed to *Pax Britannica*; the strategy he shaped and administered was designed for an international stage. His countrymen were the world's police and the world's bankers: welcomed by many powers, tolerated by others, resisted by a few. Their deployment was masterminded in London and their success depended on the greatest seaborne force in the world—the Royal Navy.

Ironically for the ten men fleeing a life of penal servitude aboard the *Frederick*, it was largely the growing British hostility to the slave trade that had sent the Royal Navy out to police the seas. The slave trade had been forbidden in British possessions since 1807—although the status of slavery still existed in certain colonies—and the British government had secured 'stop and search' agreements with most of the flags under which slavers had sailed for generations. Only Portugal and the United States refused to sign up. Thus the ships of the British West Africa station stalked the 'blackbirders' making for the Americas and the Caribbean. Along the sea-routes down which slaves had travelled since ancient times into Asia and Arabia, the ships of the Cape and East India stations were doing the same. The Mediterranean, Aegean and Caribbean squadrons were hunting down the infidel pirates who infested the waters of North Africa and the eastern Mediterranean; the China station pursued them in the South China Seas. Where the slavers did not lead British ships, scientific curiosity did, for the Royal Navy was also engaged in a mammoth cartographic project and her vessels were on a mission to measure every coastline and sound every depth for the Admiralty's charts. Simultaneously with these two great tasks, the ships and their officers performed the continual, mundane duties of communication: collecting and delivering post, parcels, despatches and secret reports; carrying officials and gentleman passengers from here to there; giving lifts to ladies who found themselves in distress in foreign parts; transporting prisoners from lonely settlements to the nearest competent magistrate; conveying to England prisoners sentenced to transportation for colonial felonies; gathering information and discreetly investigating local complaints.

Royal warships were the most expensive and most glamorous part of the naval machine, but accounted only for a small part of the British marine presence across the world. The number of men o'war was dwarfed by that of smaller royal naval craft—ketches, schooners and even cutters—and by an enormous mercantile fleet. Westminster had a finger in many diplomatic pies, the Admiralty dabbled in cartographic and military ones but the City of London, financial heart of the Empire, controlled the largest naval network of all.

Colonial possessions accounted for a part of this commercial activity but, as the need for markets had expanded, the merchant navy had spread like oil across the seas, adding links with Central America, Argentina and Brazil, the Levant, Africa and the Far East to earlier connections with North America, India and the Caribbean islands. There were representatives of City companies from Valparaiso to Shanghai, Cape Town to Jakarta, insuring, receiving, packing, storing, valuing, advancing credit, brokering and freighting, adding their inquisitive presence on land to that of the British ships on the horizon. Naval officers, commercial agents, spies, consuls, missionaries, traders, botanists, explorers, collectors and chargés d'affaires forwarded information from every continent to an administration at home that recorded, sifted, collated, sometimes archived but never forgot.

Lord Palmerston's stalwart British subject might take comfort from this vast umbrella of protection and redress but it made life tricky for British subjects on the run. Foreign administrators and traders knew the value of helping the British authorities and pirates and mutineers who had betrayed the trust of a British captain never stopped looking over their shoulder. Few British fugitives could match the promise of London's favour, or, in less sophisticated parts of the world, the crude bundles of sterling that bought information.

On 14 January, vast waters opened out before the *Frederick* on every side: the Southern Ocean to the west, with little between her and Africa; the Indian Ocean to the north, with the Spice Islands hanging above; the South Pacific to the east, with tempting archipelagos and the coast of America on the far side. Nevertheless, the threat of His Britannic Majesty's authorities hung over all of them. If these ship thieves wished to live anywhere with the comforts of civilisation, they would have to pass themselves off, as William Swallow's gang had done, as shipwrecked mariners and this would, eventually, bring them to the notice of British officials. It was for this reason that many convicts sailing illicitly from New South Wales and Van Diemen's Land went no further than the unexplored coast of New Zealand or the islands of the Bass Straits, joining the pirates and sealers whom Captain Kelly had tentatively visited in 1816. Their existence was rough, lived in semi-savagery and always on the edge of hunger; but there were no lieutenants seeking promotion to report them to the Admiralty, nor consuls to report them to the Foreign Office.

The men aboard the *Frederick* did not want such a life as this. They had decided to make, initially at least, for the harbour of Valdivia on the coast of the young American republic of Chile. This minor port seemed to offer possibilities: it was well beyond the brutish islands and no longer a colonial possession, with garrisons manned by a European military; it was too small, they hoped, to have resident consuls, and too unimportant to attract regular visits from British ships on the South America station, which patrolled the coast between Rio de Janeiro and Callao. William Swallow and his gang had wished to make South America, believing this unruly continent offered them the best chance to vanish, but they had not had enough food or water aboard the *Cyprus* to attempt the six- to eight-week crossing. The *Frederick* was better provisioned.

For James Porter, this stretch of South American coast had further attractions. A few hundred miles to the north of Valdivia was, he hoped, the family that he had once deserted and with which he now wished to be reunited. His wife, the son who must be almost a man and the farm which had once been dull now seemed a haven from misadventure. Reaching Valdivia was the first step towards reaching Valparaiso and Narcisa, and regaining the life of yeoman *pater familias*, tilling his land and sowing his seeds, which he had foolishly rejected for adventure.

To get there, however, he and his mates had first to cross an immense ocean in an untested brig built for coastal sailing. Porter was the only seaman aboard with first-hand, if distant, experience of the Chilean coast but it was Mr Barker, his captain, who assumed the post of navigator and with it an awesome responsibility. Their destination was 6000 miles away on the other side of the South Pacific, a voyage that had defeated unknown hundreds of mariners. Many of the deceptively beautiful islands strung out across this ocean, like those closer to home in the Bass Straits, were home to strange tribes of European sailors, wrecked or marooned. Some lived with inbred, speechless spawn. Luckier others had gone native with the people who found them, distressed, on the beach.

Any fears inspired by the voyage that lay before them were secondary to the dangers of their immediate situation. Before any course could be plotted for the east, they had still to clear Van Diemen's Land. During the first afternoon at sea, the wind strengthened and they were able to tack in towards the coast, aiming to skim past Port Davey out of sight of any watchmen at the government post there. At eight o'clock, the first watch was set.

Mr Fare stayed on deck, for he had taken the post of first mate. He would be ship's husband, responsible for the maintenance and management of her sails, her timbers and her bilges, the 'officer' who gave the men their orders. With his experience as 'captain of the fo'c'sle' of a large ship, the ocean voyage ahead would ask nothing of his seamanship that had not already been asked. His previous work afloat, however, would never have brought him into the officers' province of navigation and he would be no help to Mr Barker here. With Mr Fare stayed the four men of the mate's watch, one seaman and three landsmen. The job of boatswain and command of the second watch had gone to Charles Lyon, unsympathetic and perhaps unreliable, but senior to James Porter in the Harbour pilot's boat.

As the light began to fade and the spiteful west-coast rocks passed away to port, Lyon and his men went below for four hours' rest.

As they slept, or tried to sleep, the wind was strengthening. By half-past nine it had reached gale force, it was taking two men to hold the helm and Mr Fare had ordered the sails shortened. Sheets were slacked off and the main courses hauled up to the yards, where three men lashed the wildly flapping canvas in. Still the wind strengthened; still there was too much canvas aloft and the ship was heeling dangerously, her gunwales almost touching the water. An hour and a half after the second watch had gone below, they were woken and called back on deck; now the topgallant must be reefed and this long and wretched job was too much for the three men of Mr Fare's watch not clinging to the wheel. On a fully crewed man o'war such as Fare had previously sailed, reefing the topgallants might take minutes—but such a ship would have 80 men working aloft. Fare had seven, three of whom had never climbed a mast at open sea and must now do so in a gale, by night, amid spray that reduced visibility to the length of an outstretched arm. But the canvas had to come down, for they risked losing the mast or having a sail blow out, so seven wet men climbed into the main and foremast yards and shuffled along the footropes to sway above the waves and fight the canvas in. One hand clung to the handholds beneath the yardarm as the mast swayed, 60 feet up and another 40 from side to side; the other clutched and bundled up hanks of rough, thick canvas and hauled up the reefing lines that concertinaed the sail. Any who still had fingernails when they went up had lost them by the time he came back down.

Reefing the topgallants was the last act of which several were capable. Mr Barker was the first to take to his berth, unmanned by sickness. Shortly after he disappeared groaning below, Billy Shires, William Cheshire, Benjamin Russen and James Lesley turned white then green, made for the leeward rail to empty their bellies into the sea and followed their captain to their berths and a night of distress. Somewhere below, the cat curled itself into a wretched ball. Five men manned the *Frederick* through that night's storm. Empty but for her ballast and a small quantity of provisions, she had few of the barrels and crates and stores that keep ships steady in rough water. Two men at any one time had to remain at the helm, the weather 'so boisterous' that one alone could not hold the course. There was no changing the watch at midnight for those below were incapable of movement. The gale did not abate. 'We were rejoiced,' Porter recalled, 'by daylight dawning upon us without having experienced any accident.'

A reckless press of canvas had put nearly three hundred miles between the fugitives and Macquarie Harbour by the dawn of 16 January, their second day at sea. However, tearing along in a heavy swell, making ten or twelve knots even under reefed topgallants, the *Frederick*'s timbers had been working so badly that her belly had filled. It was James Lesley, recovered from sickness, who delivered the bad news. Lifting a couple of boards before coming on deck, he had found an 'immense quantity of water' in the hold.

The bilge of a ship—especially that of a newly launched ship whose timbers have not yet swelled—requires the same obsessive maintenance as her canvas but work aloft had been so great that none of Mr Fare's watch had been able to sound the wells during the night. Lesley was immediately sent up onto the wet waist of the ship to rig one of the pumps, mounted between the masts. It would not work: the valve was either defective or some lump of nastiness was stuck in its trunk. Down the hatch Lesley went to raise the bilge boards again, slither down and see what had gone wrong. Working ankle-deep in filthy water, thrown against the hull by the movements of the ship, he could not get the pump to go. It was obvious to him that there must be shavings or woodchips in the strum box, or some other of the shipyard detritus that clogs the pumps of any new ship. Staggering back on deck and over the waist, he found with relief that the starboard pump, at least, could be rigged. Had that also been defective, the voyage of the *Frederick* would have ended dramatically off the south Tasmanian coast. From now on, two men of each watch would be absorbed in the backbreaking work of pumping to keep the ship afloat. Those at the handles would be at the very least drenched in spray, and sometimes covered in the solid water that crashed over the side to knock them down. With two others lashed to the wheel, one alone of each watch of five was left to do deck duty, work aloft and keep a lookout.

Mr Barker recovered sufficiently from his sickness to come on deck later that morning and set about his navigation. He was following a primitive system. The earliest British merchant seamen leaving for the trading depots of the southern hemisphere were given simple and semi-facetious instructions: 'go south until the butter melts, then turn west'. A couple of days after the butter first softened on the plate, they turned west until they sighted the coast of South America. This—known as 'running along the parallel'—was easy enough to do. To stick to one parallel, or line of latitude, a navigator had only to keep the sun in the same place relative to his ship, checking its position each day at noon with his quadrant or sextant. If the angle had decreased, he adjusted the course to the north to bring the ship back into line; if it had decreased, he adjusted to the south. A rough count of speed was kept with a log-line and lookouts were kept at the masthead and cat-heads and flogged if they failed to spot land, a brutal but necessary incentive to stay alert. Countless ships running along the parallel have hit land before they expected; thousands of mariners have drowned because a log-line has been badly cast.

The parallels had been known and sailed for centuries. The great problem, unsolved until the 1760s, was calculating longitude. Even after a reliable method was devised, calculation required an accurate chronometer and a knowledge of spherical trigonometry, a fiendish branch of mathematics. By the 1830s, chronometers could be found on most ocean-going ships and many masters or mates had a copy of the Admiralty's books of ready-computed longitude tables, the thousands upon thousands of figures that obviated the need for time-consuming spherical trigonometrics so liable to error.

Mr Barker had no chronometer and it is unlikely, given his hasty and ill-equipped tuition, that he had learnt any spherical trigonometry. Valdivia's second great attraction as a destination was its latitude. The latitude of Macquarie Harbour is 42 degrees 14 minutes south, that of Valdivia almost the same, and Mr Barker was counting on this fact. How he knew Valdivia's latitude is a mystery: perhaps he had casually worked the conversation around to this when talking to Mr Hoy or Captain Taw; perhaps charts had been left within his trusted reach; perhaps James Porter remembered it from the old days. Barker also had a quadrant, presumably pinched from the Sarah Island commissariat, a compass, two watches (Captain Taw's and Mr Hoy's), some sort of chart (homemade or stolen), the rough knowledge of deduced reckoning acquired in Mr Schofield's night-school and a firm belief that, as their course was almost due east, he could bring the *Frederick* safely in somewhere along the 150-mile stretch between Valdivia and the island of Chiloé, the southernmost point of the Chilean coast. This faith and this rudimentary kit would have to serve in place of the sextant, the Admiralty chart, the book of longitude tables, the chronometer and the six- or seven-year apprenticeship served on any naval ship before such a voyage might be attempted. Mr Barker would be using the old ways, those of the navigators who sailed before Harrison's chronometer was tested, proved and produced. He would round New Zealand, go north until that country was out of sight, then sail east along the parallel until they hit America, or America hit them.

After seeing out two nights of gales, the *Frederick* had long since doubled the south-west corner of the island and was whistling along the south coast, out of sight of land, with strong winds over the starboard quarter pushing the boat on. Mr Barker set the new course east by south to keep them in the lee of New Zealand, protected from the winds racing across the Southern Ocean. Having done his duty, Barker crawled back to his berth, still a very sick man, and the tasks of helm, yards, lookout and pump continued with whichever men were well enough to take their turn doing so, for the change of watches was impossible in the face of the nausea on board. Porter and the others who did not suffer *mal de mer* snatched sleep where they could and did the work of ten, cursing William Cheshire, runt of a Birmingham litter, brought along because it was too dangerous to leave him behind, and the other unhappy landsmen who did not know how to manage the sheets and were reluctant to climb into the yards.

On 17 January, Mr Barker was too unwell to rise and take his noonday observation. The ship held her course. On 18 January, the wind strengthened again and Mr Fare, exhausted and concerned by the battering taken by the *Frederick*'s hull, ordered the topgallants furled again to slow her rate through the water even further. Whichever seamen were not too sick climbed the mast, crawled out onto the yards with the gale on their backs and took in the last canvas of the high sails. Now they were powered by topsails alone. For three days, the backbreaking routine continued and the wind did not change, or abate.

The rest of the men began to rise, at least for short periods, to take their turn at pump or helm but Mr Barker had not ventured on deck for the past five days. Despite the steady hand of Mr Fare, the men were growing concerned. Barker was the navigator and the ship might run well enough without him, but where was she running to? They had been out of sight of land for more days than a landsman was comfortable with, crashing on in a straight line towards an empty horizon. On 21 January, they spotted a quantity of floating seaweed ahead, a common sign that land was near. The rocks and empty beaches of the Snares Islands were invisible but tangible somewhere to the north. The South Pacific Ocean was about to open up before them and some decision had to be made about the course that would take them across it and bring them to land at the right place on the vast American coast. Mr Fare, alarmed by the men's concerns, went below and persuaded Mr Barker to be seen taking a sight and making a decision. So weak was the captain that two men had to carry him on deck and prop him up from either side while he looked at the seaweed, gathered his strength and addressed the men. 'Do not be in the least dubious as to my knowledge or capability of performing what I have taken in hand,' he said, 'for I can take you safe to South America, even although I had no quadrant on board, for I could do it by keeping a dead [sic] reckoning, it being a straight course.' The men, Porter said, 'appeared to be satisfied with this assurance', even more so when Barker took an observation, 'supported by two men to keep him steady: this afforded great satisfaction to all hands'. Job done and fears allayed, Barker was then carried below and left in his bunk.

Mr Barker's assertion was optimistic. Seamen say deduced reckoning alone is 'acceptable for one day, dubious for two and after that you're guessing', and Mr Fare, at least, must have been aware of this. 'Ded reckoning' is based on just two sources of data: the number of miles covered and the direction in which the ship is heading. The compass secured by James Porter from Mr Taw's cabin provided the ship's direction. The number of miles covered came from casting the log-line, a rope marked at intervals with knots. Once or twice in each four-hour watch, this was dropped astern and a half-minute sandglass started. When the sand had run through, the rope was drawn up and the knots submerged during the ship's half-minute passage through the water were counted off. With gales still running behind them, the *Frederick* was making an average of eight knots per hour and this, with the direction in which she was heading, should have been plotted onto the chart each day in a steady, pencil-drawn line. The cross marking their estimated position should then have been compared to that given by each noonday sighting of the sun.

But another five noons passed with Mr Barker in his berth and no sights taken and the *Frederick* was making 150 miles each day, sometimes more. She could be up to a hundred miles off her supposed position, the angle between her intended and her actual destination widening with every mile covered. Nonetheless, for nine days she ran east, her sails few and reefed but her speed between seven and eleven knots. They were still horribly short-handed: two at the helm, two at the pump, one on lookout running up and down into the yards to tweak the canvas. Again the horizon was too constantly empty, the course too constantly straight; and Mr Barker, in whose hands their safety rested, was not there. Charles Lyon took him his meals and told them he was suffering, but not in danger; but each day Mr Fare grew more haggard and the captain still did not come. The whispers started again: Mr Barker did not know how to take them to Chile; he had discovered he was not able to do what he had promised; he was hiding for fear of what they would do when they found out he had misled them. With the infernal work in her bilge, the ceaseless wind behind her and an absence on the bridge, the *Frederick* was not a happy ship.

This is what Mr Fare explained to Mr Barker below decks, exhorting him to make the effort and rise again. On the fifteenth day of the *Frederick*'s voyage, he appeared, ghastly white and thin, but determined to show the men they were in safe hands. He could take no sight that day as clouds obscured the sun. On 31 January, however, the sky was clear at midday and the ship's company watched, silent, as the talismanic quadrant was lifted and the sight taken. The same day, the wind veered and at last Mr Barker changed course. It was still an empty horizon, but a different one, and in the direction of America rather than on, endlessly, around the bottom ring of the world. The wind, though of the same strength and causing the same demon pressure on the hull, was now blowing them to a different place. Gradually, the mood on board changed and, perhaps because the motion of the vessel had eased with the change in course, perhaps because he was alarmed, perhaps because he realised fresh air was better than the stew of his berth, Mr Barker stayed on deck. He was still there, days later, to witness the 'white squall' that nearly capsized them.

The approach of an ordinary squall is unmissable: big black clouds amass before you. A white squall, on the other hand, can drop from an apparently clear sky and bear down on a vessel with no warning. This one did exactly that and it threw the *Frederick* on her beam ends, heeling over with her scuppers under water. A shudder reverberated through her as the 30-foot-long boom of the mizzen mast was torn off by the sea. Yards of split and tangled rope whipped the deck and anyone who did not jump out of their way in time. A wooden spar perhaps a ton in weight had gone over the side, pulling the ship even further over and smashing against her hull. Bringing the spar in must wait, however, for the most vital task was to reduce weight aloft: only this would allow the foundering vessel to right herself before the water reached her ports, filled her hull and dragged her under. Every man was instantly on deck. Four raced forward to climb the main mast. Two scrambled out along the middle yards and grabbed up the topsails. Others climbed further, to the topgallant yards, working against the spray and the winds to release first the heavy pin that anchored the yards to the mast, then the halyards, and send them, sails, spars, ropes and all, whistling and collapsing down to the deck. The lower yards, where men clung with one bleeding hand, skimmed the water. When two other men took the final reefs in the main mast topsail, the *Frederick* groaned, heaved herself slowly out of the water and righted.

Despite her reduced canvas, she was still scudding along far too quickly. There were panicky shouts in the cockpit: the men said she was being forced, she could not take it—she would go again on her beam ends or the water forced in below would overwhelm them. Mr Fare would not shorten sail further, for he was more frightened by the water behind them than that in the brig's belly. It was a bold decision: many mariners would have chosen to take off the last of the canvas, put out a sea anchor to slow the ship down and sit out the squall. But with heavy seas running dead astern, Mr Fare knew the *Frederick* was in danger of being 'pooped': engulfed by a mighty wave which would crash over her from behind, shift her bodily sideways and leave her to be capsized by the next. To prevent pooping, the *Frederick* must keep ahead of the sea; to keep ahead of the sea, she must have way through the water; to have way she must have canvas aloft. Fare kept his authority, ordering the frightened men to concentrate on bringing in the spar over the side, splinting it and hauling it again into position. The squall blew itself out but the gales did not. They blew every day for the next nine days.

At least Mr Barker was now taking his sight every noon. It was 19 February when he lowered the quadrant and called a meeting. Their position according to the sights was badly out compared to that given by a fortnight's deduced reckoning. If they continued on her present course, they would meet South America somewhere on the inhospitable coast of Patagonia rather than the estuary of

Valdivia. He had decided they must alter course several degrees to the north. This brought the wind, which had been just over the quarter, uncomfortably round over the side and they would have to sail thus, broad-reached, until the wind shifted or they made land. The broad reach, always rough on a square-rigged ship, increased her already perilous speed and forced in more water, which had to be painfully pumped back out. The man at the helm on the first watch after this alteration was Charles Lyon, who should have known better. With green water sluicing across the deck, the brig heeling at an alarming angle and the canvas again threatening a blow-out, he ordered the men to slacken the sheets. This, releasing the pressure of the wind on the sails, turned the *Frederick* back the crucial few degrees that Mr Barker had changed. This action gave the ship a more comfortable ride but it took her back onto a course to nothing. Guessing the reaction of the other seamen to what he had done, Lyon was careful to bring the brig back onto Barker's course at the end of his watch and handed over to Mr Fare without comment. It was at midday, when Mr Barker took his next sight, that the error was discovered, for many miles had been lost whistling along under four hours' easy wind. James Porter had to be restrained from rough justice when, 'taxed with this gross neglect of duty, (the rascals) told the truth'. Had not others interceded, he would have given Lyon 'a short passage over the side' but in the end the man was let off 'with a caution not to do the like again at his peril or he should certainly die'. Lyon was a seaman; he had no landsman's excuse. Grievances were building.

They thought they were a week or so out from the American coast when someone saw a vessel on the starboard bow, the first spotted since leaving Macquarie Harbour. One man went up the main mast with the glass in his hand and confirmed that a small boat was hull-down on the horizon, making her way south. All hands were immediately ordered on deck with arms and ammunition.

On the lonely routes of the oceans, any two ships passing after weeks, perhaps months of isolation, would 'speak each other'. One crew would raise their ensign to signal their nationality, the other would raise theirs in reply and then the bunting would be brought out to semaphore messages from deck to deck. If the senior officers of both ships were unhurried, they would visit to exchange greetings, news of winds, currents, channels, port duties and correspondence. Many naval wives received their husband's news through the kindness of American merchantmen sending it on from Rio, or Frenchmen from Madras, or Hollanders from Batavia. Those vessels who did not raise a courteous ensign in greeting across the waves were concluded to be pirates, who sailed under the flag of no country; or the small boats of the uncouth—sealers, whalers, fishermen, more concerned with trade than the exchange of courtesies. The ten men of the *Frederick*, standing on deck, waited to see what the other craft would do. If she hoisted her ensign, the *Frederick* could not answer her, for there was no flag, nor 'bit of buntin', on board, and then the other crew would certainly 'come alongside and make themselves inquisitive'.

This was what the men dreaded. They were indeed pirates; and if the other vessel were British, her crew would be under an obligation to seize her, or, failing that, to report her position and probable course. Then one of the British frigates cruising the South American coast would be set on her tail, the authorities on land alerted and the future suddenly would become far more dangerous. They waited to see a flag hauled from deck to masthead, and loaded their muskets in anticipation for, had the unknown seamen indeed proved inquisitive, they 'were determined', said Porter, 'to run on board of them, capture them or die in the attempt, for we knew if we were brought back Governor Arthur would hang us to a dead certainty'. The other boat drew level and passed. Soon her stern was visible: she was clearly no more interested than the *Frederick* in interrupting her voyage for society. The muskets were unloaded and carefully put away; the tomahawks laid back in Captain Taw's arms chest.

Three days after the stranger had slunk past them to the east and about a quarter of an hour before dark, 'all hands imagined they saw land ahead'. It was 25 February. There were excited shouts for Mr Barker but he would not have it. He said 'it was impossible, for that by his reckoning we were exactly 500 miles off Chili [Chiloé]'. Mr Fare agreed with the men. He knew the weaknesses of deduced reckoning as well as he knew the signs of land approaching: birds, weed, a different smell, the mass of dark clouds that sat above the mountains, visible just inland of the Chilean coast. He also knew they were down to their last two pounds of meat and the biscuit was wet. The bilges were overflowing, for tired, wet, hungry men could not pump effectively. Mr Barker's misgivings were overridden, the men so eager that they did not demur at this reversal of authority. Two went forward to keep a lookout from atop each cat-head. At about ten o'clock, they were sure they could see land. Mr Fare ordered the brig hove-to, there was the irritating whump and slap of empty canvas and the *Frederick* gently slowed. She had brought them 6000 miles through gales and rough seas. They had been six weeks and a day at sea.

One part of their voyage to freedom was nearly over. No one back in Van Diemen's Land knew which direction they had taken, nor whether they were not all dead meat on a beach. Suddenly, the second part of the adventure was approaching: the moment at which other people, strangers, entered the story. These strangers might be suspicious, possibly hostile, certainly curious. No word could have arrived from Hobart of the escape of convicts but, sooner or later, the British authorities would spread the news to every part of the world. When the next English frigate of the South America station tacked into whatever port they were approaching and the next lean English officers called on the governor, no one must hark back to the arrival of ten shipwrecked Britons and connect them with those sought by London.

As the *Frederick* lolled, hove-to, they rehearsed 'a plausible yarn'. However, when James Porter took it among himself to cross question them on the details agreed, he 'found they were all upon their guard with the exception of Cheshire, who became quite indifferent as to what he should say'. Hindsight may have inserted this conversation into Porter's adaptable imagination, but he was not the only one to distrust Cheshire, for the boy had never become one of the gang. 'I told the remainder of my companions,' Porter recalled, 'it was my opinion that if they pinched [arrested] him, he would come it and hang the whole of us.' When Porter then declared passionately that the youth must die and cocked a pistol to deliver the sentence, Mr Barker—who had, after all, been Cheshire's master and felt some responsibility for him—reached up from the cabin and dragged Porter from the top step of the ladder. Cheshire was not malicious as much as weak, loose-mouthed and easily scared. Barker begged Porter not to shed blood, gripping him round the ankles, and promised him that Cheshire would be put ashore at the first land they came to. Porter swore and struggled, but would not go so far as to kick his captain in the face. Coaxed back down into the cabin, he was 'so vexed', however, that he threw his pistol, still cocked, on the floor and it went off, resounding in the small space and frightening everyone. Curses were unleashed in his direction. Cheshire might betray them from weakness or self-interest but Porter might do it first from intemperance. Anger was suppressed by emergency for their situation required immediate action.

They had always known they would have to scuttle the *Frederick* to present the appearance of shipwrecked mariners but several miles still separated them from what they thought was the coast of Chile and they had hoped she would take them a little further in. An increase in her groaning and weeping told them it was prudent to launch the longboat now. Some rigged blocks and tackles to the yards to raise the longboat from her chocks. The carpenters added another fore-and-aft plank to give her more freeboard, for, with the heavy swell, and once loaded with ten men, a cat and supplies, her gunwales would be too close to the water for comfort. They also added a half-deck, covering her bow over to provide a little cabin and keep out the worst of the spray. The fitted tarpaulin that Captain Taw had had made for the whaleboat was altered and stretched and lashed down over the longboat's cockpit. The yards were swung out to square. Down she went, dropped astern to lollop in the swell, but in lurching against the hull of the *Frederick*, the upper plank just added was damaged. Four men jumped aboard the longboat, balancing against the waves, to slot the mast into its shoe, attach the boom and bowsprit and lace on her two sails. As they finished, they were hailed by frightened voices: while the launch was being made ready, no one had been at the pumps. Four feet of water had surged into the *Frederick*'s bilge while they were rigging the longboat and when she drifted too far from the *Frederick*'s flank, her half-laced sails flapping, the men left on board called their mates back in alarm, fearing the brig would sink before they could leave her. The remaining provisions were speedily lowered in along with fresh water, guns, ammunition, compass, a spyglass, two coils of inch rope, an anchor and 35 fathom of cable. They poured nails into her bilge as ballast and handed down the cat to crouch in the bow. As night came on, the men left the *Frederick*, her channel plates nearly under water. They knew she would sink by daybreak.

Their arrival near Chiloé, and their survival of rough seas and high winds in a virgin vessel, was a testament to the skill of the navigator and first mate. Porter knew it. Years later, when he came to write of his experiences, the other men were referred to by their surnames but Mr Fare and Mr Barker, the two who had commanded his obedience and admiration, are never mentioned without their respectful prefix.

His affection, however, was reserved for the little brig that had brought him so far.

'I never left my parents with more regret,' Porter wrote, 'nor was my feelings harrowed up to such a pitch as when I took a last farewell of the smart little *Frederick*.'

6

The Coast of Araucania

While the *Frederick* was wearing the storms of the South Pacific, the nine men abandoned on the shore of Macquarie Harbour struggled through the north-western bush. With one of their leaders sick and in need of constant support, and the other hungover and enraged, this was an arduous journey. They were wet through and exhausted when they reached Circular Head but, because of the generosity of the supplies left by the mutineers, all nine survived. Officers of the Van Diemen's Land Company took them in. By 6 February 1834, they were back in Hobart Town and faced with the task of breaking the news to Governor Arthur. He did not take it well. The previous year had been an embarrassing one for authorities: one man had sneaked on board an American brig in March 1833, nine had stolen the 25-ton schooner *Badger* in July and not yet been located and four more had stowed away aboard the *Bee* in September. The ten aboard the *Frederick* meant the new year was starting badly and brought the number of those who had recently absconded by sea to 24. Governor Arthur had no doubt at whose door to lay the blame for this latest disaster.

All government-employed seamen in the colony were required to act in accordance with a book of 'Instructions issued to the Masters of the Government Vessels'. These were designed specifically to ensure convicts were never given the opportunity to seize command of a vessel and, wrote Governor Arthur to London, had been 'utterly neglected', by Captain Taw, 'or the occurrence never would have happened'.

Captain Taw might have made imprudent choices in selecting the crew but blaming him for negligence in not sticking to the letter of the *Standing Orders* was unfair. Item VII provided that 'as a full and efficient crew has been provided for the vessel, no assistance will be required from the prisoners in working the vessel'. This not being the case aboard the *Frederick,* other regulations could not be observed. Item IV required the prisoners 'to be constantly kept in heavy double irons', with a twice-daily examination to see if any attempt had been made to remove them—impossible when the men were both convicts and crew. Item V, that 'no axes, crow-bars, hand-spikes or any thing that could be used as an offensive weapon, is to be left within reach of the prisoners', again was impracticable if the men were to work efficiently on deck, and the command that they were 'always to be kept before the windlass' was useless when duties required them aft.

Nevertheless, Governor Arthur had decided that Captain Taw must take the blame and the tone of their interview may be deduced from his biting despatch to Lord Stanley, Secretary of State for the Colonies in London.

'I have the honor,' it said, 'to report the final abandonment of Macquarie Harbour.' He went on:

I regret, however, to state that this has not been effected without loss. The Commandant, on breaking up the Establishment, was under the necessity of leaving ten convicts of the least objectionable character in order to complete and bring up, a new Brig which had been building. These men were placed under the charge of the Master of the Vessel, the Builder, with their two assigned Servants, who could be depended upon, and who acted with great determination and good conduct, together with the Mate and a Guard consisting of a Corporal and 3 Privates, a force more than Sufficient had the most ordinary Vigilance been used, to have kept them in perfect subjection. This, however, had not been the case. The Master, who had long been on the Station, entrusted with the most dangerous and responsible appointment of Pilot at Macquarie Harbour, from that degree of culpable security which is always the Parent of danger, took no precautions. No Sentry was posted. He himself was down below and two of the Soldiers were fishing, at some distance from the Vessel when the Convicts suddenly rose, seized the Soldiers arms and, after a short struggle, were in a few minutes in possession of the Vessel and after landing the Guard and other Parties proceeded to Sea on the 13th ultimo in a S S West direction and probably made for New Zealand.

A Board of Inquiry was convened and copies of the *Standing Orders* immediately sent out again to all colonial skippers.

At the same time as this flurry of correspondence left the governor's secretariat, more practical measures were being discussed to chase the *Frederick* and bring her back. It being presumed that she was heading for New Zealand, a letter was drawn up and sent to Mr Busby, the honorary British Resident there, with Black Book descriptions of the ten men aboard her. The same descriptions were enclosed with the London despatch to be forwarded to the Lords Mayor of Dublin and London and circulated to British port authorities: heights, colouring, scars, distinguishing features and tattoos of the ten missing men.

It seemed a stroke of luck that a British man o'war, HMS *Alligator*, was at anchor in the River Derwent and an urgent letter was rowed out for Captain Lambert, begging the honour of his attendance at Government House. Here, Governor Arthur informed him of the loss of the *Frederick*. She had been out three weeks, he said, would by now have made the coast of New Zealand's South Island and was probably hiding among its dozens of bays, her crew looking to join up with some colony of fugitives and sealers. If the *Alligator* went immediately, she stood a decent chance of running the stolen ship to earth, bringing the pirates back and saving Governor Arthur's battered face. This was why he strongly suggested to the captain 'the expediency of at once undertaking so important a service'.

Captain Lambert, however, was no Jack Aubrey. 'Under the instructions which he had received from the Admiral on the [East] Indian Station' (which covered Australia), Governor Arthur explained to London, 'Captain Lambert felt differently in adopting this course without previously proceeding to New South Wales.' In Captain Lambert's view, Lieutenant-Governor Arthur's instructions were insufficient and had to be confirmed by his superior, the Governor of New South Wales in Sydney, even though, as Arthur acidly pointed out, 'it was evident that any delay would necessarily diminish the chance of eventual success'.

As HMS *Alligator* dropped anchor in Port Jackson, Sydney, and her captain awaited confirmation of Governor Arthur's now useless orders, the fugitives in their longboat were approaching a coast 6000 miles away. Even close in to land, the sea was still wild and the waves still high; the boat, with ten men, stores and a dismal tom cat aboard, was 'uneasy'.

An hour after leaving the *Frederick*, as they sailed north keeping a good offing from the cliff, the wind rose and the longboat 'shipped two seas': two great waves crashed completely over her and nearly sent her down. A big sea had begun to run behind them, threatening to flip the longboat stern over bow. Until it veered or lessened, four men of each watch would have to sit in the stern-chains, hoping their weight would counter the pressure of the malicious waves beneath. 'This of itself,' said Porter, 'was sufficient to kill the strongest men', and there was no relief from it. Had they headed still further in, they would have found a gentler sea, but it was too risky to approach, by dark, the unknown rocks and reefs of the South American coast. Thus through the cold night they ran parallel with the shore, straining in the darkness to make out the shape of an unending 'bold, high tract of land' without shelter for shipping, bays or villages or any sign of human habitation. The rocks came sharp and perpendicular to the water, iron-grey and jagged, and the only living things among them were the seabirds. It seemed a hard and unfriendly place, as inhospitable as the west coast of Van Diemen's Land.

It was a cruel night, running under a lone foresail because of the strength of the wind. When the sun came up, the men were relieved to see the cliffs were giving way to fields and the shore, 'close aboard of us and covered with a rich verdure', was beginning to resemble the green and pleasant land of Valdivia that James Porter remembered. The sheets were hauled in, the boat was turned shorewards and the pressure of the sea beneath them eased.

They ran northwards again for most of that day, resting, eating little for provisions were low, and staring towards the shore for sight of a river mouth or sheltered bay; perhaps, with great luck, a harbour. Mid-afternoon, the coast ahead seemed to yawn into a wide, shallow bay and Mr Fare altered course to approach. In the lee of land, they rigged the mainsail. An hour and a half later, they found a reef which would stand between the boat and the north-westerly wind, anchored, and set foot on South American soil.

The cat streaked past them, wild with pleasure to be at last on land. The men went more cautiously, not knowing if there were

Indians about, or feral whites, for these, too, were sealing waters. The shores of the bay were rich with shellfish, ready to be gouged off the rocks, 'which to us', wrote James Porter, remembering his hunger, 'was a luxury'. They slept that night on shore, newly full of protein, with a two-man watch 'to prevent wild beasts or any intruders coming upon us unexpectedly'—or, a likelier and more dangerous possibility, to raise an alarm if the capricious winds changed and the reef no longer sheltered the boat. Should she be forced on shore and wrecked, their situation would be truly desperate. Early next day, the cat came nosing among them, mewing and, some of the men thought, coaxing them to follow him. But the others dismissed this fancy, rose late, drank fresh water and spread themselves over the rocks to gather shellfish to eat for breakfast, then stalked and killed a seal for lunch.

They called for the cat to come and eat some seal, but he did not come. They called again as they finished their meal but still he did not appear. It was early afternoon, and they were anxious to leave and continue up the coast to find civilisation. Some prepared the boat, others packed up the seal-meat; no cat appeared at these sounds of preparation. Ten men beat gently at the edge of the bush, calling puss! puss!, but the tom cat did not come. They left him a hunk of seal-meat on the beach and pushed off.

At the mouth of the bay, they hauled up the sails; the wind freshened and two hours' 'smart sailing' took them to a point of land running a long way out to the north-west—so long that it took several hours to weather, with the prospect of 'another dismal night at sea' should there be no bay on the northern shore. Disappointment gripped them, and renewed fatigue, when they scanned the far coast and saw that there was not; only several hours' running before the wind. Eventually, as dark was coming, they came upon a cove, its mouth flanked by two large rocks. On the leeward ledges of these

Portrait of a convict: no photo or painting exists of James Porter; however, he would have been dressed in convict garb similar to this. The defiant stare was probably also shared.

After being sentenced to transportation for the term of his natural life in 1823, Porter began his journey in a prison-ship *(above)* and was then transferred to the *Asia* with 249 other men for four months and two days' sailing to Hobart Town *(below)*. Here they would wait in Hobart gaol for assignation to their new masters.

Four months after his arrival in Van Diemen's Land in January 1824, Porter climbed over a wall in Hobart Public Barracks and escaped. He was on the run for eighteen days. When captured, the guards brought him in and flogged him one hundred times.

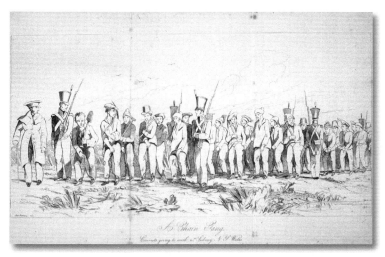

After his second failed escape in 1826, James Porter was sentenced to six months on a chain gang such as this.

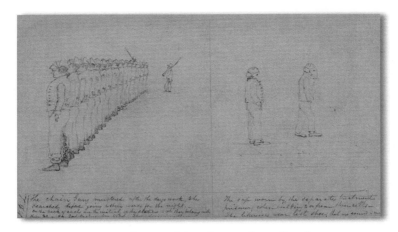

From sunset to sunrise, Porter and the other members of his chain gang were locked into huts far too small for their number. At half-past five each morning they were called to muster then marched to the quarries. At the end of the day another muster marched the gang back to their cramped quarters.

After numerous escape attempts Porter was charged with being 'illegally at large under a Second Conviction'. In March 1830, he was sent in chains to Macquarie Harbour.

The Gates.

Sixteen days out from Hobart, Porter arrived at Hell's Gates – the sardonic convict term for the harbour mouth at Macquarie Harbour. It was one of the most dangerous harbour entrances in the world.

Macquarie Harbour was expensive to run and its costs were not covered by the production of its ship and timber yards. Its greatest asset was its isolation – it was a place of ultra banishment, perfect to break the spirit of any inveterate bolter.

GOVERNOR ARTHUR.

A portrait of Governor Arthur: the man determined to find and punish any man or woman who dared escape from Van Diemen's Land – the ship thieves would not be forgotten should they choose to follow their plans and attempt to find freedom.

The Van Diemen's Land Company sought to open up the lonely west coast of Tasmania to grazing. It would create more opportunities for the remaking of men gone bad – but this meant Macquarie Harbour would cease to be the perfect place for convicts. Port Arthur was to take its place.

While working on the last Harbour-built vessel a plan was hatched to steal the *Frederick* as soon as she was launched. Like many before and after, James Porter and his fellow ship thieves chose to face the perils of ocean travel to escape the brutal reality of life as a convict in Van Diemen's Land.

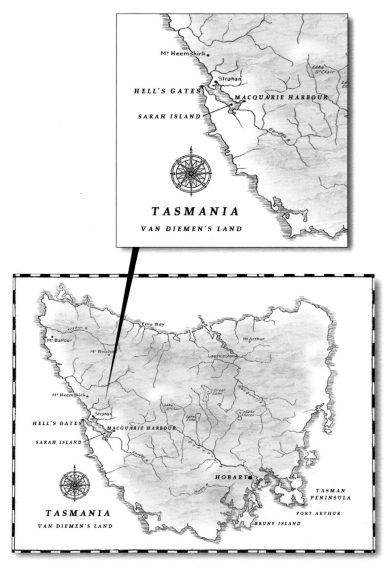

A map of Van Diemen's Land. The starting point for James Porter and his fellow ship thieves.

was a colony of plump seals. Four landed and saw a stream of fresh water to go with the easy meat of seal. Jubilation: it had been worth the long run. However, those who went to reconnoitre were soon back with the disturbing news that an Indian hut was nearby. Immediately, the boat was hauled off the beach, Macquarie Harbour-style. Three manned her and seven went to check the hut. It was deserted, and appeared to have been so for some time. Nevertheless, they spent that night not vulnerable on the beach but squashed close together aboard the longboat, anchored in the bay 'a good distance from either rocks or beach, with a view of securing ourselves from any intruders'. A watch of two was set as darkness came and the eight other men sank into exhaustion.

It was 1 March 1834. Early in the morning, the ten men 'surprised a seal and killed it' and cooked the flippers, heart and liver for breakfast. Fortified, they skinned the beast, conserving the rest of the meat, and nailed the pelt over the plank that had been stove in when the longboat was hoisted from the *Frederick*. After breakfast, they got under way and were soon making seven knots an hour, bouncing across the water before a fresh breeze, running from bay to bay up the coast 'in the expectation of finding inhabitants'. They found none that day, dropped anchor late in one of the endless, shallow, disappointing bays which studded that coastline and nearly came to grief. Within half an hour, the changeable wind had begun to drive a large swell onshore and the boat had pushed upon her anchor and torn it from the seabed. Finding themselves suddenly drifting onto the rocks, they managed to kedge the boat across the water and behind a reef which gave shelter from the north-westerly. There she swung, uncomfortably, until morning.

The next day the swell continued heavy in the bay but there was almost no wind, so they had to take to the oars and row along the shoreline, still looking for signs of human life. The previous day's pattern repeated itself: bay after wide bay, with nothing and no one there. Again it was late afternoon when hopes were raised, for a bay larger than the others had been seen about four miles ahead and Mr Fare was optimistic. He judged, he said, 'by the look of the land that there must be some port or other near'. Half an hour later, 'we anchored in the safest boat harbour we had yet been in'. There were no humans running down to the waterfront to see who was putting in, nor huts, nor fires nor any other sign that there was a settlement here but several small saplings had been recently cut down around the bay, 'doubtless', they thought, 'to make masts for whaleboats'. A lovely river sparkled to one side. They had another meal of seal-meat on the lonely beach that evening and slept ashore.

The men woke on 3 March determinedly cheerful, all sure they would meet inhabitants at the next port they came into. 'Our spirits being elevated with these hopes', they stood along the coast with a good breeze in their favour until, at midday, a long promontory came into view. Sailing back in towards land on its northern shore, they were surprised by a familiar sound from the shore. 'All of us in the boat were instantly as silent as the grave; not an individual could be heard to breathe, as we intently listened that we might again hear the welcome sound, fearful, lest our ears had deceived us.' Where there was a cow, the likelihood was that there was a person. The beast mooed again, and this time a human voice answered it, 'the most cheering sound any of us had heard for many, many days and caused satisfaction to gleam on every countenance'. Closer in, they saw human figures around a fire. Those on shore had not noticed the small boat and 'being surprised, gave a kind of yell' when the men aboard hailed them. The sounding line went over and came back: the water was too deep to anchor; they would have to continue along the coast until it shallowed. Desperate not to leave the fire too far behind them, they sounded every few yards and brought up a couple of miles further down, in 22 fathoms.

'The whole of that night we kept awake,' recorded Porter, 'conversing with each other.' The men were too excited to sleep and also too scared, for they knew how changeable the winds of this coast were and that the small reef in whose lee they had anchored would not save them should the lightest onshore wind spring up. At first light, they put oars to rowlocks and pulled back to where they had seen fires. A vast spread of kelp lay between them and the beach, too thick for oars. They pulled themselves in along it. Nearing the stony shoreline, they saw Indians among the boulders, each with a knife in his belt, each watching the white men heave. Were they friendly? It was decided that five would stay on board the longboat and five, armed, would go on shore, for 'we considered if we met with a hostile reception it was far better for five of us to lose our lives than ten of us'. They were right to be cautious, for this was dangerous territory.

The men watching from the boulders were *mapuche*, known to the Spanish as the valiant Araucanians; the only native people in their vast American empire to have obliged the conquerors to come to terms and observe a frontier. For nearly three centuries, they had confined Spanish settlement to above the river Bío-Bío, 250 miles to the north. A century ago, Spanish and *mestizo* (mixed-race) settlers had begun to creep south from there, gradually taking over Indian territory, and now the frontier of Hispanic settlement was at Valdivia.

British and French diplomats in Chile had recently shared their worries about the dangers to European mariners on the Araucanian coast. Mr Rouse was British vice-consul in the nearest British consulate to Valdivia, in the town of Concepcion. He had recently tended the crew of the *Saracen*, an English brig grounded on the rocks of Chiloé, whose crew had been led to safety by the Araucanian

Indians who found them there. With no other country being diplomatically represented so close to the shipwreck coast, it was also Mr Rouse who bore the brunt of helping distressed mariners of other flags and it had taken up a lot of his time. 'It is a concern,' he had therefore hinted to the French consul-general in the Chilean capital, Santiago, 'common to all nations whose whale-vessels frequent those dangerous and inhospitable shores, to accustom the Indians to respect the lives of unfortunate beings by storms thrown upon their territory: to render them humane by the allurement of gain, by making it evident to them that more advantage is to be derived from the preservation than from the destruction of Europeans.' The French consul agreed that Indians helping Europeans must henceforth be rewarded and details of this inducement were sent out by means of trackers and traders but the scheme had not worked quite as hoped. In June 1833, the French whaler *Rose du Havre* was wrecked in a storm. Two of her crew were detained by the Indians who, wilfully or innocently misinterpreting the consuls' hand of friendship, were demanding a hefty ransom for them. The rest got away and struggled into Valdivia overland, although 'death', wrote one, 'would have been a thousand times sweeter' than the sufferings they endured along the way.

The men aboard the *Frederick*'s longboat did not know of the unfortunately worded offer recently made to the local Indians, nor of their habit of bearing down on shipwrecked sailors and stripping them silently and swiftly of every possession; still, all Englishmen knew the heathen foreigner was not to be trusted and they watched the approaching natives with a wary eye.

The Araucanians came down to the beach, making gestures and, the men thought, asking questions, but in a language they could not understand. The men closest to the Indians started making 'hungry' gestures, raising scooped hands to their mouths, chewing the air and patting their stomachs. The Araucanians could not—'or would not', said Porter, hungry and impatient—understand, but continued their incomprehensible questions. The bewildered fugitives started to make animal noises, 'the cries of sheep, pigs and bullocks', but grunts and moos had no effect either. One man among the Indians, extremely tall and wearing ornamented clothes, appeared to be the chief. Back went one of the *Frederick* crew to the boat, returning promptly with a hatchet. This Porter offered to the tall man; 'he brandished it over his head and then beckoned us to come ashore'. It was not an attractive invitation. Several were reluctant to accept it but finally Billy Shires volunteered to go 'and take with him some needles and thread' and Porter and three others stepped forward to go with him. The boat was hauled further in on the weed, a loaded pistol given to Shires and the landing party jumped ashore. Immediately, the rest pushed the boat four lengths back. From a safe distance, they watched their five comrades on the beach achieve some sort of communication and disappear in the midst of the Indians. In a few minutes, the beach was deserted.

The five ashore had found the natives friendly but still struggled to communicate. James Porter knew some Castilian and the Araucanians knew the word *Valdivia*. In reply to a tentative *cuanto lejos*? one of the women held up three fingers and said 'leghos'. Three leagues—nine miles; they were nearly there. 'I returned to the boat overjoyed,' said Porter. A few trinkets—'buttons, pins and needles'—were given to the obliging Indians, 'which pleased them much'. The rope was freed from the kelp, the sails raised and the longboat set once more on a northward course, towards a distant promontory pointed out by the woman. That afternoon, they weathered the final point and at last saw the huge, sheltered bay, large enough for a fleet of ships of the line, several battered forts, the silvery River Valdes disappearing distantly from its head and an island rising from its waters. James Porter had already visited this estuary, fourteen years ago.

He had married his Narcisa at a turbulent moment in the history of Chile, when the Patriots, risen and fighting for independence, took on the forces sent by Madrid to beat its most remote colonial possession into submission. The swashbuckling British officer Lord Thomas Cochrane had been recruited by the Patriot command to take charge of an infant Chilean fleet of six ships, blockading the Spanish ships in Callao harbour and fighting them along the coast. *Leones marinos*—'sea lions'—was the name the Chileans gave to the British seamen, enthusiastic for battle and loot, and it was stories of their derring-do that had seduced James Porter from his wife's farm. Working aboard a troopship, Porter had seen the forts of this estuary when Admiral Lord Cochrane swooped down to dislodge the Spanish from them and 'liberate' the town upriver in the cause of Chilean independence. It had looked very different then, with Patriots camped on the hill behind and Spanish resistance manning the guns to pound Cochrane's schooners in the bay. Now there was only gentle activity, the movements of Chilean harbour officials in small boats in and around the forts and the unloading of goods from trading vessels of many nationalities.

In the longboat, the men hove-to in order to discuss how they must approach matters. Mr Barker opened the arms chest and gave a half sovereign to every man on board. All clothing in the boat was divided equally among the ten, except Captain Taw's and Mr Hoy's watches, which Mr Barker kept for himself. There was a last swift rehearsal of the story which they had adopted on leaving the *Frederick*, and the longboat was steered towards the battery of the Corral, the largest of the estuary's forts. As they approached, they saw people running down to the landing place to point out where they should bring the longboat in. A crowd had gathered by the time they landed, several soldiers among the throng, eager to help the foreigners haul their boat as far up the beach as possible. With the ebb of the tide, the longboat was soon high and dry and it was the moment to try out their story before an audience.

They were survivors from the wreck of the brig *Mary*, they told the group that helped them ashore, five of them sailors and five passengers. The *Mary* had put out from Liverpool in December and was on course for Chiloé when the vessel went down, her captain and others still aboard. The ten had managed to lower the launch, pulled away—'in order not to perish by the dashing of the waves'— and made for the coast. From this point of the story, they could stick to the truth: the nights spent sleeping aboard the longboat, the many points weathered and disappointments suffered, the feeding on seal-meat and the discovery of the Indian village. They were heading for Valparaiso, they said, and the international community there which would help them, but 'the passengers [having] their fears of so long a voyage in so small a vessel, requested the Sailors to leave them at Valdivia'.

Their story was given credibility by the wrecks of the *Rose du Havre,* the *Saracen* and the other European craft broken up on the Araucanian rocks and the people at the fort that night were sympathetic and eager to help. When they learnt that the 'passengers' were carpenters by trade, they told them of a vessel on the stocks upriver in Valdivia, where, they said, there was 'plenty of work to be had'. It was easy enough to see that there were no British Royal Naval vessels in the harbour. Why not stay for a while? It was as good a place as any and it was true that the five non-seamen aboard had little desire to spend more time at sea. They could easily get upriver to the town of Valdivia, said their new friends, a canoe could be hired for five dollars to take them there. When the Chileans eventually went to bed, the ten held a conclave. Early next morning, they split into two groups. After seven weeks together, through danger and unpleasantness, dispute and comradeship, Billy Shires, William Cheshire, John Dady, Benjamin Russen and Mr Barker were to go one way, upriver to the shipyards of Valdivia; John Jones, James Porter, Mr Fare, James Lesley and Charles Lyon would continue up the coast. 'We bid them farewell,' said Porter, 'for we never expected to see them more as we intended to launch our boat the next day and get under weigh for Valparaiso where I knew if my wife children and friends were alive I should remain during my life and return thanks to God that I did not founder on the rocks of despair.'

Late in the afternoon, the canoe with the five landsmen aboard disappeared in the direction of Valdivia, fifteen kilometres up the river that wound from the head of the bay, above swirls and bends and sandy peninsulas and little islands which protected the townsfolk and their fertile fields from attack. Among Valdivia's inhabitants was a handful of foreigners. One of these was a young man known as Cockney Tom, of enigmatic past, who had wandered in several years ago, married and stayed. One of the means by which Cockney Tom supported himself in his Valdivian life was by doing small services for the *intendente*—the local governor—or the port authorities, or whoever else needed a bilingual fixer. When the five 'shipwrecked' carpenters appeared in their hired canoe that day and tried to tell their story in terrible Spanish, he was called in to translate. It was with Cockney Tom that at least one of the five men, later that afternoon, went drinking in a Valdivian tavern and slipped into indiscretion. Later still, all five were surprised by soldiers of the town guard and taken to gaol in the *cuartel*—the town's barracks.

The seamen, still downriver at the Corral, were unaware of this development. For them, departure for Valparaiso had not been as simple as they hoped, for they had missed the tide and could not get the longboat off. They would have to wait another twelve hours.

What was there to do but party that night as they had done the last? There was congenial company, tales to be told and embroidered, men with guitars, ladies to dance with and barrels of liquor. As the carpenters—or one of them—sat in a bar on their first night upriver and told too much to Cockney Tom, the seamen were celebrating, 'for the remainder of that day and night', with the Patriots. No wonder they 'slept over late' the next morning, nor that their awakening was unpleasant: once again, Porter opened bleary eyes to see men with muskets straddling his head. Questioned overnight, the men in Valdivia had told of the five others left with the Patriots of Fort Corral and the men with the guns had been sent to get them. Sore-headed and apprehensive, the seamen followed their comrades upriver aboard a patrol boat. That evening, they, too, slept in the *cuartel*, seat of town government, and were not permitted to see the other five. Several Chilean officers called during the evening but all were evasive; none could, or would, tell the men why they had been arrested. They were only 48 hours into their new life, and things had already gone badly awry.

During that uncomfortable third night, one Sergeant Orutea was detailed to guard the foreigners. This sociable man arrived in the early hours with some 'aquadent', locally made firewater. 'I offered him a dollar,' Porter said, 'but he refused it until I pressed upon him very much.' It was from Sergeant Orutea, invited to stay, chat and doubtless sample his own wares, that they learnt—Porter translating—of Cockney Tom and the drinks he had offered their carpenter comrades. Porter wrote a brief note to Mr Barker, stating 'that [his] suspicions fell on Cheshire'—that it was he who, deliberately or unwittingly, had betrayed them. Sergeant Orutea stuffed the note into a bit of bread and trotted off, his night more full of incident and company than any for a long time, and came back with another bit of bread and a note in reply. Mr Barker, cooler-headed than Porter, 'thought it was only their suspicions and could not believe that any one would be so mad' but Porter remained 'uneasy'.

They were in the cells for a week. Courteous officers came and went. Mr Fare, as supposed mate of a shipwrecked vessel, was given an allowance of one dollar a day. Charles Lyon, as supposed bosun of the same, received half a dollar and the other eight were given a quarter each. With this money, they bought their own food and drink, cheap in that bountiful place. Their comfort was inquired after but still no explanation was given for their detention. Seven days after the men with the muskets had woken them in the Corral, there was a commotion across the yard and the unmistakeable sound of Frenchmen with a grievance. It was Sergeant Orutea who came with the news: the new arrivals were the captain and crew of a wrecked French whaler—the same, as would become apparent, that had not spoken them when they sighted each other on the ocean a couple of weeks ago.

The *Confiance* had been driven aground during an early-morning storm on 7 March, about 100 miles south of Valdivia. Their ship's boats smashed to pieces against the side of the whaler, Captain Olivier and his crew had roped themselves ashore. One was dragged away by the waves and presumed drowned. While they were attempting to save items floating up onto the beach, they were attacked by the *mapuche*, who 'stripped them of everything including clothes', took them away and held them for a day and a night. When the *cacique*, the Indian chief, arrived, they were released but given no food or drink, and no directions to help them on their way to the nearest European settlement. On 15 March, news of Europeans wandering in the jungle reached the *cuartel* and a posse was sent out to bring them in. Thus, the second troupe of wet, hungry men to claim shipwreck in a fortnight arrived in Valdivia, and was detained in the cells. Captain Olivier, however, had a packet of papers in waterproofed canvas to prove that he and his crew were bona-fide mariners in distress and the Frenchmen were only briefly neighbours in the gaol. Within a couple of days, they had been taken in by families of the town and Vice-Consul Rouse of Concepcion was on their case.

Shortly after the French had passed through, the reason for the Britons' long confinement became clear. The *intendente* had been a fortnight from home, on 'a party of pleasure to the Imperial, a place where some civilised Indians resided', and in his absence, the case of the suspicious foreign sailors could not be heard. The day after he returned, officers came to the cells. They were to be taken to the Government Palace and interrogated.

The room into which ten ill-shaven and resentful men were ushered was a large and splendid one, dominated by an enormous, polished table. At the head of this sat the governor, Don Fernando, 'a fine, noble looking fellow' and a cluster of officers. The ten mariners stood in a group at the bottom end. Neither the governor nor any of his officers knew English. The first man to be introduced therefore was an Englishman, Captain Lawson, a schooner master who had rescued the men of the wrecked English brig *Saracen* off the Araucanian coast five years ago, and a smuggler—a fact overlooked when, as now, he could also perform the role of gentleman interpreter.

Names were asked for, and aliases given, along with an explanation of how they had come to arrive in a small boat in the bay.

James Porter (now James O'Connor) was spokesman for the convicts. The first questions, concerning provenance, destination, nature of leak and so forth, he answered satisfactorily, following the agreed story, but Don Fernando, however mild his manners, was tenacious. An official came forward with items confiscated from the longboat, among them the *Frederick*'s glass and the brass sheaves of her blocks, all stamped with the mark of His Majesty's Government. Why was this? the governor inquired. 'I accounted for them,' said Porter, 'by stating that the British Government often have a sale of old stores and all things were sold with the Government mark in them—and that the owners in the Merchant Service would not trouble themselves in taking them out.' It was a good explanation, but 'still there was something doubtful in the mind of the Governor. "Call Thomas,"' he said, '. . . and the redoubtable Cockney Tom made his appearance.' Asked by Don Fernando to swear publicly 'if all he had stated privately to him was a fact', Cockney Tom agreed it was, and retired.

The Governor was silent for a few minutes then said, 'Sailors you have come on this Coast in a clandestine manner and though you put a good face on your story I have every reason to believe you are pirates and unless you state the truth between this and tomorrow at eight o'clock I shall give you orders for you all to be shot. Take them away.'

It was then that James Porter—at least in his own recollection— called a magnificent bluff.

> 'Avast there . . . a word with you upon the subject. We are sailors shipwrecked and in distress expected when we made this port to have been treated in a Christian-like manner not as though we were dogs, is this the way you would have treated us in 1818 when the British Tars were fighting for your independence and bleeding in your cause against the old Spaniards—and if we were Pirates do you suppose we should be so weak as to cringe to your Tyranny, never! I also wish you to understand that if we are shot England will know of it and will be revenged. You will find us in the same mind to-morrow we are in now, and should you put your threat into execution tomorrow we will teach you Patriots how to die!'

As elsewhere in Porter's narratives, however, the prominence he accords himself in retrospect does not quite square with other accounts.

Over the next few hours or days, the truth of the foreigners' circumstances came out in further interrogations, although exactly how, and by whose confession or mistake, is unclear. The Chileans would not have had much difficulty in prising from them the true story: cracks had already appeared in it before they were taken to the Government Palace. Some had claimed that the captain of the fictional *Mary* 'had perished in the boat at the stern of the Brig'; others, 'that they had left him on board because he persisted in remaining there, contenting himself with pointing out to them the course they ought to bear to meet with land'. Some said they landed at a port called 'Castro' to repair their battered longboat, others had given it a different name, or did not recall landing at all.

James Porter, as previously, would blame disclosure on William Cheshire alone, claiming he begged that evening to be taken before the *intendente* for a confidential interview and there told the whole story, in order to save his own skin. In this version, when news of Cheshire's confession was brought to the gaol, Porter told his companions 'that there was only one way to baffle Cheshire's expectations . . . that if we went before the Governor the next day, we should state the whole truth to him—to do away with Cheshire's evidence and include him in the number'.

When the summons came to the palace and the *intendente* asked them if they had anything to say against Cheshire, Porter therefore told him the whole of the circumstance but also stated that 'we would rather have died than stated anything of our affair but our motive in so doing was that Cheshire should not escape but share the same fate as us, and as we had stated the facts of the case we hoped he [the governor] would not put Cheshire's name down in his despatches as the approver, he said he could do as we wished and that he should face as the rest. We all thanked him. The Governor then turned to Cheshire and said, "Had you been a South American instead of what you are all the forces I command could not have kept the rabble from tearing you to pieces.'"

Porter's allegation could have been justified and William Cheshire may have been the weakest link in a chain of tired, scared, confused men talking for their lives. However, what is even more likely is that bits and pieces of the story leaked from various of the ten, contradicting each other in solitary interviews, encouraged by insinuations that others had already confessed all. Whichever way it was told, and by whom, very soon the Chilean officers knew every detail of the men's story: their real names and convict status, the name of their scuttled ship, what they had done with her officers, where and when they had stolen her and what they had suffered during the voyage. Their cover was entirely blown. By the beginning of May, just over a month after they had landed with hopes of anonymity and freedom on the Araucanian coast, a report of their presence and identity had been sent to the Chilean Secretary of State for Foreign Affairs in the capital and their story had even been written up in the local newspaper.

Any further attempt at dissimulation was useless. They had confessed and their confessions were recorded in print. Their identity was public knowledge and it was only a matter of time before the British consulate was alerted. A change of tack was needed. Boldly, they appealed to Don Fernando to support and forward a petition to the Secretary of State for Foreign Affairs, requesting asylum in Chile on the basis of the inhumane treatment they had received from the British government. Pleading the wretchedness of their plight and the harm which must befall them were they to be handed over to the British navy for repatriation, they threw themselves on the mercy of the Republic of Chile and hoped it would be sufficient to protect them from the might of Britain.

7

Playing Cat and Mouse

Beyond the town, the Rivers Calle-Calle and Las Cruces joined to flow to the sea as the River Valdes, pooling and parting, splitting about islands and rejoining, turning back on itself, cutting a last channel, deep and narrow, and finally forming a shallow and beautiful bay some three miles wide. Mountains, lakes and volcanoes spread away behind the rivers and a mile downstream from their confluence was the little town of Valdivia, encircled by tributaries. Every square and street of low wooden houses was cooled by rain and apple blossom; along the banks of the streams, a profusion of trees grew down to the water, where pelicans nosed in the weed. Among those who walked barefoot on the tracks between the houses were people familiar to the men of the *Frederick* from their first encounter with the *mapuche* further south. They had already witnessed women wrapped in blue blankets and men whose dark faces bore a strange resemblance, wrote a more educated visitor, to portraits of Charles I: 'a sombre cast of depressed intelligence that at once said, "we are restrained, but not subdued" and a sinister though resolute glance, which seemed to ask whether we were also come to try for a share of their country.'

Fifteen thousand people lived in Valdivia. The town had once been among the proudest of the Spanish American possessions. Founded in the sixteenth century, it had been named for one of the mad, fanatical, brave conquistadors who took half the world for Castile, marching south through the endless deserts of Peru in the search for slaves and silver, settling finally in the fertile Central Valley. 'This land,' Pedro de Valdivia had declared three hundred years ago, 'is such that for living in, and for settling, there is none better in the world.' It had bristled with Spanish fortifications, been taken by the Dutch and the *mapuche*, reconquered by the Spanish and made to bristle again. More recently, the people of Valdivia province had been the last in Chile to disavow Madrid and yield to the republican guns of the Patriots. Now, they were no longer colonials, but citizens of their own republic. Still the vast tract of land to the south of their city, claimed as republican territory, was largely unknown to them.

Valdivia was the southernmost European town of any size on the west coast of South America. The town's isolation, on the edge of the vast continent, was not unlike that of the rawest Australian townships crawling up the coast of New South Wales and clinging to the edge of newly settled Port Phillip Bay. Valparaiso, the country's principal port, was at least four days' sailing up the coast. Santiago, the capital built on a mountain plateau, was a month's overland travel to the north and between that city and Valdivia were large and magnificent lands only nominally Chilean, in truth under unchallenged Araucanian rule. Through this, the overland couriers rode to deliver their mail and despatches. One hundred and seventy miles to the south was the tiny frontier town of Osorno and beyond there were Europeans on the little windswept island of Chiloé, but then came nothing. Nothing but the unending, unknown, unfriendly coast of Patagonia, where earlier sailors had reported monopods and monsters, centaurs, sirens and the famous mariners' myth of 'men whose heads do grow below their shoulders'.

The *Valdivianos* lived well. Immediately behind the port, tree-covered high hills attracted clouds that kept their land fertile and the temperatures low. Behind these lay the plains, *los llanos*, soft and green, stretching all the way to the cordillera of the Andes. Here were the farms and plantations, worked by Negroes and Amerindians, and those great estates known as *encomiendas* descended from Don Pedro's land grants, where the local variations of slavery, serfdom, servitude and dependence were played out. In the town, commerce revolved around the river and the sea. Valdivia's boatyards were in constant activity, for any family of means had a share in some vessel or other; warehouses, suppliers, carpenters, agents and all the usual secondary trades were thriving on premises and quays along the miles of river bank, and boats of every size were on the stocks and slips beneath the apple blossom. This was the town where the ten men of the *Frederick* hoped to make their home—some, permanently. James Porter wasn't one of them. He still yearned for his Narcisa.

With their pleas for compassion temporarily answered, the men were released from gaol. The day after, the governor Don Fernando, rather taken by his new guests, invited them all to the launch of one of his own vessels in the river. Work thereafter was not hard to find, for Valdivia could absorb any number of skilled boatbuilders. It seems to have been humanity on the part of the governor, along with the desire to profit from the men's boatbuilding skills and perhaps admiration for their courage, which prompted him to lend his support to their petition and release them on parole while this was being considered in Santiago. Asking them only to report once a day to an officer at the palace, and advising them to repay as soon as they could the money they had been advanced while in gaol, Don

Fernando told them they were free to leave the *cuartel* and find lodgings and work while they waited for Santiago's response. Nine immediately found accommodation with families or employers in town. William Cheshire, however, asked for the protection of the governor, who found odd jobs and some sort of residence for him about the palace. He was given a guard to accompany him whenever he left the palace grounds 'and I hope you in particular, Porter', Don Fernando said, 'will not molest him'.

News of the men's presence and identity quickly spread around the small town. Soon it had been carried by riverborne gossip to the yards and quays in the estuary, where bigger vessels moored and unloaded. People pointed and peered at the boats where the men were working and their adventures were told and retold in inns and salons. It would not be long before some of these Chinese whispers reached the ears of British seamen and British administrators further up the coast.

The nearest British vice-consulate was Mr Rouse's office in Concepcion, 150 miles away. The British Consul-General, Colonel Walpole, had an office in Santiago but spent most of his time in Valparaiso, where it was easier to maintain contact with passing British ships. At Rio de Janeiro, five weeks' sailing away, a large naval establishment commanded the fleet of floating gaols, post offices, courtrooms, freight carriers, news-gatherers, surveyors, spies and sweepers which kept a British eye on the coasts of South America. When one of these various representatives of King William IV heard of the ten runaway convicts washed up in Valdivia, no one could doubt that he would spread and act on the information—and when he did so, a fugitive's plea for help was unlikely to prevail against a government's request for extradition.

Don Joaquín Tacornal, Chilean Secretary of State for Foreign Affairs, had been perplexed by the petition that landed on his desk towards the end of April, accompanied by a pleading letter from the governor of Valdivia. Ten self-confessed British criminals appeared to have won over his subordinate, found gainful employment and been taken to the town's bosom. Tacornal sent official notification to Colonel Walpole of the presence on Chilean soil of ten distressed Britons claiming asylum but the colonel had already read the remarkably thorough account of their story in the local newspaper, the *Monitor Araucano*, to whose editor the men's confessions had been disclosed. Realising the importance of the information, Colonel Walpole ordered a translation of the article to be made for Viscount Palmerston. He attached a note to his despatch:

Your Lordship will perceive that certain Individuals, 10 in Number, a list of whom is also enclosed, presented themselves on the 9th of March last at Valdivia, stating that they had been shipwrecked on the coast of Chiloé—that the veracity of their account appearing very doubtful, a further examination was entered into, the result of which was a declaration on their part, that they were Convicts from Van Diemen's Land having taken forcible possession of a Government Vessel called the 'Frederick' and made their escape from that Colony, thereby not only rendering themselves liable to a further Penalty for escape from Transportation but adding to the Catalogue of their Crimes, the Act of Piracy.

This last being considered by the Government as an Act forming one of the list of atrocious crimes punishable by the Laws of all Civilised Nations, it has directed that these Individuals shall be placed in safe Custody until further Intelligence tending to confirm their Innocence or Guilt shall be received.

I have considered it my Duty with a View of procuring such Intelligence by the earliest means to transmit direct to the Lieutenant Governor of that Colony a Statement of the Circumstances and to request the requisite Information; but I fear that the Opportunities of Communication are too rare to lead me to hope for a speedy acquisition of that knowledge which will alone enable me to apply for the surrender of these Prisoners by the Government of this Country with any chance of Success.

This despatch, written on 25 May, was held ready for the next ship to call at Valparaiso en route to Rio, from where it would be sent on to London. There was no Australia-bound ship in the harbour to take Walpole's letter on to Governor Arthur, nor was any expected soon. His request for 'requisite Information', carried via Rio and Sydney, would not arrive on Governor Arthur's desk in Van Diemen's Land for another four months.

Meanwhile, Secretary Tacornal at the Ministry for Foreign Affairs was unsure how to proceed. On 20 June, while Colonel Walpole's letter to Lord Palmerston was ploughing across the Atlantic in the despatch bag, a second letter left Tacornal's office for the British Consulate:

> In consequence of the government having received a Petition subscribed by the Individuals, (in which they, representing the deplorable situation in which they find themselves, beg for asylum in this country) and as the Government of Chile is still ignorant of the nature of the crimes for which they were condemned to that place of banishment, (Van Diemen's Land) it cannot determine as to the future fate of these unfortunate men; neither is there any other channel through which it can expect to arrive at the truth in this matter except through you. I have therefore to beg that if you are already in possession of any of the particulars that you will be pleased to communicate them to me for the ends desired.

The colonel, in possession of no more of the particulars than he had been when contacted a month previously, and with little expectation of a ship bearing answers from London or Hobart Town coming in soon, could only beg for patience. He was, he replied, 'feelingly alive to the wretched situation of these miserable men, but at the same time, he cannot but be sensible, of that which rigor and justice demands, and he therefore trusts that the Government of Chile will admit of their continued confinement until their guilt, or innocence, of the atrocious crime of which they have confessed their criminality can be accurately ascertained . . . If he could not yet provide proof of the offences for which they had been sent to Van Diemen's Land, their guilt of piracy was surely clear'.

Nothing, however, was as clear to the Chileans as it was to Colonel Walpole and what the colonel understood by confinement was very different to that understood by Don Fernando in Valdivia. That gentleman interpreted the meaning liberally, sending for the ten men to tell them that a preliminary answer had come from the Ministry for Foreign Affairs in Santiago of which his understanding was that, pending Colonel Walpole's production of any evidence against them, not only was he—the governor—'to protect us, since it was the whole of the inhabitants' wish' but that 'we were at liberty to marry if we thought fit'.

Despite the swift detection of their fraud—passing themselves off as shipwrecked mariners—the men's faith in Chile as their lucky destination seemed as if it might yet be justified and they took swift advantage of their new freedom. They had already gained some celebrity. The nature of their arrival, their exciting criminal past, the hardships of their ocean crossing and their Britishness set them apart. Don Fernando was monitoring their employment—some of them were at work on his own vessels—and deducting money from their wages 'in order to economise the expense of their maintenance' whilst in gaol. His obvious sanction of their presence did no harm to their professional or social prospects.

None of the ten could settle entirely to his new life until an answer to their petition for asylum came from the Supreme Governor in Santiago. Until then, they did not know whether they would have to up sticks again and disappear abruptly into the night, leaving new friends and employers behind. As weeks went by and no British warship appeared in the bay with orders to collect them, their confidence began to grow. The townsfolk continued to treat them well and, it seemed, were confident their petition would be granted. All—except William Cheshire, still in residence in the governor's palace, still afraid to come out—began to integrate well into their new community, learning Spanish, earning decent money, finding themselves long-term positions at local yards.

Some were integrating in more personal ways. Their new home was not a town of pomp or great riches or grand buildings; there were not the long streets of inns and brothels that hosted sailors in the great ports of Valparaiso and Callao, further up the coast. Valdivia offered a modest way of life but for men starved of domesticity, used to the brute male life of barracks and camps, this was one of its attractions. The gentle entertainments of the market, the central plaza after Sunday mass, the evening *paseo* and the girls who came to watch them work were seductive. Despite having left a wife and two children in Cheshire, Mr Barker (under the name of Benjamin Smith) married a local woman he can have known only a matter of weeks, the governor and his wife present and beaming at the wedding feast to toast the new couple. Billy Shires, now Billy Jones, married and almost immediately his new wife, Catalina, a similarly recent acquaintance, was pregnant. James Lesley (or George Fortune)—also with wife and child in Wales—and Benjamin Russen (James Price) followed them into hasty matrimony and even William Cheshire (William Williams) became betrothed during one of his furtive sallies from the governor's palace. This happy parole was not at all what Colonel Walpole had envisaged.

James Porter, having been briefly employed on one of the governor's boats, found work with one 'Don Lopez', a Valdivian merchant who had invested in a quantity of valuable skins bought from hunters in the interior. These were waiting at a spot about 50 miles inland and Don Lopez's problem was to find an economical way to bring them to the harbour and ship them out. Between Valdivia and the depot that held the skins were several stretches of river where the rapids ran fast. Lopez had already lost cargoes and lives. This was a job for a coxswain trained in the spiteful waters of Macquarie Harbour: any man who had steered a boat past the pilot's spit, over the bar and through Hell's Gates would not be deterred by South American whirlpools. After reconnaissance in a small boat, Porter reported he would pilot a 16-oar launch and 'if the Peons [oarsmen] would do as I told them there would be no fear'. Don Lopez accompanied him on his first trip—'which caused a great many Ave Marias to escape the lips of his wife for our safety'— perhaps wondering if his skins were quite safe in the hands of a known criminal, whatever his coxing prowess. Should this Englishman use the skins to finance a bolt into the interior and away from possible British pursuit, Don Lopez stood to make a substantial loss. Their voyage inland was uneventful; coming back, however, the rapids were so fast that Porter was obliged to unship the rudder and replace it with a long oar, a method of steering that gave greater flexibility but demanded greater skill. It was, Porter claimed, 'the first time of a cargo coming home safe' and the first of several trips.

On a small farm outside Valparaiso, 250 miles to the north, who knows if Narcisa read the name James Porter in the *Monitor Araucano* and heard a small, sour bell ringing in her head? Whatever his original intention, Porter had not skipped his parole and gone north seeking his wife and son, as he had imagined he would during the dark days of the ocean crossing. He had access to boats, working for Don Lopez, a job that allowed him to be out of town for several days at a time without anyone raising the alarm and the professed desire to see his dear ones again. True, his escape would land the kind governor and the other men in trouble and might bring about the 'safe custody' which Colonel Walpole wished for. Gratitude to Don Fernando and loyalty to his mates, however, were no longer the only pull exerted by Valdivia, for it is at this point that the name of Narcisa ceases to enter his narrative, never to return, and those of Doña Inés Asuncion, or 'Lady Asencion', and her slave girl Antonietta, begin to creep in instead.

First mention of the high-spirited Chilean widow comes in Porter's typical cockerel style.

> There was a lady of Don Lopez's acquaintance called Donna Inez [sic] Asuncion, who begged as a favour from Lopez to use his interest in her behalf in persuading me to go and live at her place during the time the slaves were making Cyder [cider] to protect her and her little son and property. The question was asked [of] me if I would go. I felt for her and consented not knowing the spitfire I should have to deal with. I took leave of my friends and they parted with me as if I was their own child and begged of me to return as soon as the Cyder was completed.

Porter left Valdivia when the first fallen fruit lay on the ground beneath the trees and the faint smell of fermentation permeated every house. In a town of apple blossoms it was not surprising that cider-making was more than a pastime. He arrived at the Asuncion ranch, many miles upriver, by dark. The next morning, Diego, Doña Inés's small son, introduced the new foreman to the house-slave, Antonietta, 'a handsome girl about 16 years of age'. This unfortunate had been captured by the chief of another tribe when her father was away, had seen her mother killed, and had then been sold on, at the age of twelve or thirteen, to Doña Inés, her price set at 'a cow and a hatchet'. The lady of the house had at first been kind, she said, but had lately turned against her. Twenty-three field slaves were gathered outside the house and introduced to their new master, Porter's first working day began and Doña Inés left on a visit. This was the pattern of the first few weeks of his employment and, during the hours that Doña Inés was away from home, Antonietta and other slaves began to tell him stories of the lady's character 'which caused me to wish to leave'. She was wild-spirited and hard, they said; she treated her slaves badly; she was viciously jealous.

About a month after Porter had arrived, Diego came to him one morning in distress, telling him his mother was punishing Antonietta in the barn because Porter had been 'too kind' to her. He found the girl there with her thumbs 'tied up to a cross piece . . . with her toes scarcely touching the ground', cut her down and berated Doña Inés when that lady came running. Doña Inés immediately tied Antonietta up again, Porter cut her down and then 'the lady ran to a drawer and rushed at me with a carving knife'. There ensued a nasty fight, which ended with Porter bringing down a chair on Doña Inés's head, knocking her senseless and lodging her comb in her skull at the same time. While she lay unconscious, he packed his bag and left, taking Antonietta with him.

He had intended to take the girl to Don Lopez's house in Valdivia, where she would be better treated, but they did not get that far, for there was no canoe for hire until the next day. They found lodging with the town magistrate instead, where Doña Inés, 'a sad spectacle for the comb had stuck in her head' came knocking the next day and promised good behaviour. That time, they agreed to return. From Porter's own record there are hints that he was receiving more than food and board from the fiery widow and the cause of her jealousy was probably well-founded.

A little later, it was rumoured that Indians had threatened to attack the small European settlement near Doña Inés's ranch and a posse of soldiers was sent up from Valdivia to guard them. With little to do until the attack came, some of the soldiers formed the habit of dropping in on Doña Inés for company and a glass of cider. One siesta time, however, when the lady was sleeping, 'a black sergeant, a Corporal and two privates'—all drunk—came not for society but 'for the express purpose of plundering the place of the Cider and aquadent'. This part of Porter's tale is most believable: Chilean soldiers were no better or less inclined to drunkenness than their counterparts elsewhere and Doña Inés's brewery was a magnet. However, the bar-room tapestry of fisticuffs and heroism into which Porter wove the ensuing brawl stretches credibility.

Diego brought news of the strange men's arrival and Porter emerged from the house to see them forcing the door of the storeroom. 'I rushed upon the nearest,' he said, 'and knocked him down with my fist.' Despite being half-blind and five foot two, and having only a 'long hunting spear' thrust into his hand by Diego, he then single-handedly defeated the three others, all armed with guns. When they ran away into the bush, he turned to bind the wounds of the sergeant, who begged him not to mention the affair to his officer. Porter agreed and thought the matter finished until, that night, he discovered the vengeful three who had got away had found 'a Peon, made him half-drunk and gave him some money to kill me with his sealing knife'. The assassin was to hold his knife under his poncho, ask Porter for the loan of his pipe, throw it to the ground so Porter would bend over to retrieve it, then attack. Instead, Porter disregarded the shattered pipe and punched him in the face, toppling him into a cider trough which capsized him 'and in trying to save himself he exposed the open knife, I flew at him and took it forcibly away from him while his companions were gazing at me . . .' When the lieutenant was informed of all this, he sentenced the sealer summarily to death and the sealer's poor, wretched wife (with babe in arms) came to throw herself at Porter's feet.

'"Don Santiago O'Connor," she said, "I have been given to understand my husband is to be shot tomorrow for attempting your life when elevated with liquor," her sobbing choked her utterance when she presented me the baby. I took the child from her and kissed it, when she asked me, almost stifled in tears, whether I would save the child's father, by forgiving him or leave him to perish, herself would then be a widow and the child fatherless in the wide world . . .'

When the man was brought for trial, Porter, chest expanding, interceded and begged the favour that the court pardon his attacker:

> They all appeared to be amazed when at last the Captain [Porter meant the lieutenant] spoke. Here is a contrast of great magnitude [directing his discourse to the trembling sealer] it was only yesterday you were contriving to take this generous Englishman's life, and now he is supplicating to save yours, for shame of you, and from this moment never never forget the villainy on your side, and the compassion of the foreigner on the other, go, quit my sight, and ever bear in mind, it is to this generous sailor you are indebted to your life . . .

James Porter did not spend all his time being a gentle knight up-country but returned sometimes to the town for the companionship of his mates and some carpentry work along the river. It was, by now, common knowledge in Valdivia that the British Consul-General had been told of the foreigners' presence and identity, yet still they enjoyed Don Fernando's favour and work was plentiful. John Fare (aka John Thompson), John Dady (George Riley) and John Jones (Patrick Welsh) had all been recently taken on to fit out a sloop, property of Don José Maria Hernandez, an acquaintance of the governor. James Porter, newly back in town, easily found work aboard a barque moored further up. Others were employed in workshops in the town. By the terms of their agreement with the governor, all ten were still required to report once a day to an officer but Hernandez's boat was too far downriver for a daily trip to the *cuartel* to be practicable. The three Johns lived aboard, Hernandez had undertaken not to let them ashore unsupervised and Don Fernando accepted his promise.

Also in the Valdes estuary at that time, below the sandbar and guarded by local troops, was a large foreign trading brig. The *Ocean* was owned and commanded by one Captain Theodore West, whom Porter recalled as a Swede but was in fact British, presumably sailing under a Swedish flag. Captain West was in trouble. Officers from the Corral had found contraband goods aboard his vessel and she had been confiscated and put up for auction, the proceeds to go to the port authorities. The captain faced ruin and the news of his misfortune buzzed round town. He made fruitless trips to the port office to plead for the release of his brig and on his return from one of these, desperate with worry, he was quietly approached by Mr Barker.

Of all ten ship thieves, John Barker had best and soonest integrated into Valdivia, his wedding given the seal of approval by the governor and his lady and plenty of well-paid work offered to a man of his skills and new connections. Mr Barker was also, however, perhaps the most intelligent of the ten, and the wariest. The good life—the new wives with swollen bellies, the cider and sunshine—and kind words from Don Fernando might have seduced the others into tranquillity but Mr Barker knew that it was only a matter of time before the Royal Navy came to find them. When Captain West found himself in trouble, Barker was ready to seize the opportunity. He proposed a solution to the captain: for the price of a passage away from Valdivia—where, it did not matter—he would assemble a crew and 'take [the brig] from under the Battery or perish in the attempt'. Captain West agreed to consider it and nine men met (not surprisingly William Cheshire, still living in the governor's palace, was not invited) and discussed Mr Barker's proposal. Some had made no ties to Valdivia beyond a decent wage and a good life—the sailors John Fare, John Dady and John Jones were three of these. They packed their kit and prepared to slip away, convinced by Barker's arguments. Billy Shires's wife was pregnant. Packing was not so easy for him. All waited. A couple of days later, they heard that Captain West had raised $2000 security from foreign merchants in Valdivia and the *Ocean* had been released.

The Swedish brig, now ready for legitimate departure, was anchored under the forts in the bay, ready for a start on the Monday's morning tide. Whether Captain West knew it or not is uncertain, but all nine had now come round to Barker's way of thinking and were still planning to be aboard her when she left. The sloop aboard which Johns Fare, Dady and Jones were working was already well-placed, being at anchor just beyond the sandbar that straddled the mouth of the river. The other six would have to cross the bar to reach her. The night before the *Ocean* was due to sail, the men stole out of their lodgings in Valdivia, took an empty dinghy from the quay and rowed a silent nine miles to join their mates.

They arrived at low tide to find a strong onshore wind, with a 'foaming surf' raised across the sandbar. They did their best, 'pull[ing] for their lives' to pass, but that night not even a dinghy crewed by men from the Macquarie Harbour pilot's boat could cross the bar. Eventually, they backed their oars in the river and waited. At dawn, they strained their eyes, saw a commotion on the distant decks of the *Ocean* and knew she was getting under way. Still the men in the dinghy could not reach her, but the three aboard Hernandez's sloop could. In the first light, the stranded six watched the others dive from the sloop and haul themselves up the gratings, cursed their luck and pulled as fast as they could back upriver. They made it to work that morning 'fatigued and vexed, with very little heart to work'.

When news of the three men's escape came upriver later in the day, going first to the governor's palace and then swiftly around town, the seven left behind held their breath and waited for retribution. Permission to live with families in the town must be revoked at least, they thought, taking Billy Shires from his pregnant Catalina and keeping James Porter from his comfortable up-country billet at Doña Inés's farm. Each day the remaining ship thieves looked over their shoulders for soldiers coming with orders to confine them in the *cuartel* but no one came. Don Fernando remained friendly, their work was not curtailed and no curfew was imposed. Yet, surely, such a slap in the face of the governor's kindness could not go unremarked and this betrayal must result in some withdrawal of his trust? The escape of the three men had left the remaining seven exposed and fearful.

The men never discovered the fate of John Fare, John Dady and John Jones, their companions in pain in Macquarie Harbour and in peril on the ocean crossing. After another change of identity there were many possibilities. A life spent in some South American shipyard? A change of career and a life among cattle, employed as peon by a descendant of one of Pedro de Valdivia's gang; or among fruit, employed by a hard-working Spanish or Italian immigrant farmer; or the adaptation of some small trade—cobbling, brewing, building—in a town far from the consulates and the coast? If so, perhaps their descendants are still there, in the rich South American mixture of blood and names. Maybe, instead, they hid out along the coast, slinking up to Callao to board clandestinely some homebound ship with sympathetic seamen or an uninterested captain, and a return to an English life lived discreetly, head down, in Bristol, Liverpool or London.

8

The Blonde and the Beagle

When Consul-General Colonel Walpole was told of the men's escape from Valdivia aboard the *Ocean*, he was as furious as Governor Arthur had been on hearing of the escape from Macquarie Harbour nine months earlier. The flight of the three Johns confirmed all his suspicions about the 'safe Custody' in which the Vandemonian fugitives were being held and his reply to Secretary Tacornal's letter was curt. 'Recall[ing] to His Excellency's recollection' an earlier promise that 'the Chilian [sic] Government had given directions that the individuals should be detained at Valdivia with all possible security until the nature of their Crimes should be ascertained', and having since that time 'had no reason to expect any change in those friendly intentions expressed by His Excellency', he had been astonished to hear that 'in consequence of the laxity of their imprisonment', three had been allowed to escape. Determined to investigate independently the circumstances in which they were being detained, the colonel summoned to the consulate a naval officer just arrived in Valparaiso.

His Majesty's Ship *Blonde*, 74-gun frigate on the South America station, was a ship of fine pedigree: fighter against the French, Pacific explorer, in her time the bearer of royalty, now under the command of the elderly but still formidable Commodore Mason. She had come to Valparaiso two months before, on one of her regular runs from Rio de Janeiro round the Horn and up to Callao. On reporting to Colonel Walpole, Commodore Mason had been given custody of three British citizens suspected of involvement in a murder in the Galapagos Islands. These he had put in irons and taken north to be sent on to London from Callao, where ocean-crossing ships gathered. On his return to Valparaiso, the skipper of an American brig had come aboard with an Englishman whom he suspected of deserting from the British Navy. This unfortunate, too, was taken aboard the *Blonde* and conveyed to Callao and transhipment for Britain. Entering Valparaiso a third time at the end of October, the commodore was asked to call again upon Colonel Walpole. This time, his task was a more delicate one than conveying suspected felons up and down the coast, for the colonel wanted him to take an independent look at the conditions in which the Vandemonian fugitives were being detained in Valdivia.

On 18 November, therefore, the sentries on watch at Fort Corral saw the unusual sight of a British frigate, ensign flying, come tacking into the bay. 'Fired two Guns at intervals,' noted the *Blonde*'s officer of the watch in his log, 'and hoisted Jack at the Fore. At 3.00 observed the Forts and Flag Staff at the entrance.' At a quarter-past six in the evening, the *Blonde* 'came about Gonzalo Point and opened the harbour', where she 'shortened sail to the Topsails, Jib and Diver'. Immediately—'at 6.18'—a small boat arrived from the fort to ask her business. The Chilean officers had to wait: it was not until 6.20, punctiliously recorded, that the crew 'let go the Anchor in 10 fathoms . . . and furled sails'. Retaining one Chilean officer on board, the commodore sent the boat back to the fort. A little later, a second small boat pushed off from the *Blonde*, this one sent 'to forward the

Mails', in doing which, the officer noted without comment, 'she was fired at by the Fort, and returned in consequence ...' James Porter, hearing later of the 32-pound shot sent over the British cutter's mast, assumed it had been fired in solidarity with the town's adopted foreigners. Whether this was the case or not, it persuaded Commodore Mason not to hurry his Chilean hosts.

'The Mails' were few: there were not enough British interests in Valdivia to warrant a regular mail drop there. No one of the *Blonde's* company, despite her years on the South America station, had ever visited this harbour. On this occasion, the mail consisted of one special delivery for the governor Don Fernando from Secretary Tacornal, reluctantly written under pressure from Colonel Walpole.

Six of the ship thieves were in their lodgings or wives' houses in the town and William Cheshire was in the Government Palace when soldiers came to round them up on the night of the *Blonde's* arrival. The soldiers could not or would not tell them why they were being brought in to the *cuartel* and several unpleasant hours of speculation passed. Was this a belated reaction to the escape aboard the *Ocean*? Had Don Fernando confined them in preparation for handing them over to the British? At about midnight, Don Fernando himself came in with a letter written in English, just brought up by canoe from Fort Corral. He could not read it; he asked the men to translate. It 'stated', in Porter's memory, 'that Commodore Mason, of the *Blonde* frigate, had received information that several Englishmen were in Valdivia, who had come on the coast in a clandestine manner, and that he would wish them to come on board the frigate and give an account of how they came upon the coast.'

When Don Fernando asked if they were willing to do so, they answered a definite no, sure that once the commodore had them, he would not let them ashore again. "Very well then," apparently replied Don Fernando, "I shall send the Commodore a letter stating I will send a boat for him and he shall be conducted to my palace where he can have an interview with you but I will not allow another person to accompany him." My companions thanked him and he said "if they force their way up I will send you all away in to the interior and let the sealions find you if they can."'

Aboard the *Blonde*, they waited for a reply. With a light wind and fine weather the next day, the commodore ordered clothes and hammocks to be brought up and washed. Still no boat came out from Fort Corral with a reply to his request. A little later, his officers 'exercised a division at quarters and a Party of Small Arms', possibly with an eye to the previous day's 32-pound challenge. Later still, they fired a salute of thirteen guns, which was returned, and should have been fired before. When the answer eventually came from the pliant *intendente*, the *Blonde* raised her anchor without reply and made for Valparaiso to report to Colonel Walpole.

Hearing that Commodore Mason had not been permitted to interview the men, and had even had his cutter fired on when delivering the request to do so, the colonel dictated an icy letter to Don Joaquín Tacornal. Feeling, he wrote, 'that it never can be the wish of the Chilian [sic] Government to protect individuals suspected of Crimes execrated and punished by all civilized nations, or that even any facility for their escape should be offered by those who have the guardianship of them', he concluded that the unwonted freedom of the British subjects in question could only be 'the result of a want of Vigilance on the part of the Authorities of Valdivia'. Having diplomatically offered Tacornal this let-out clause, he got down to business. He requested—'and [felt] himself justified in the expectation'—that the Supreme Government would now . . .

institute such an enquiry as may elucidate the mode and circumstances of the escape of the three Prisoners . . . and may ascertain the degree to

which the charge of negligence on the execution of his Duty may attach
to the Officer into whose charge they are committed, and that the degree
of punishment apportioned to his transgressions may be imposed, and
that further directions may be given to enforce the greater security of
the remaining Prisoners until that intelligence can be received which may
clearly demonstrate their Guilt or Innocence.

If Commodore Mason was prevented from investigating, the
colonel wanted to be sure that someone else was going to.

The Chilean government, however, did not accord the matter the
same priority as the British colonel and it took repeated and
increasingly testy requests before an enquiry was set up into the
flight from Valdivia. It reached a gentle conclusion. Having taken on
her cargo in the estuary, the board of enquiry eventually decided,
the *Ocean* cleared Valdivian customs, obtained a licence to put in at
Chiloé and departed. She never arrived: the licence must have been
a feint. A few hours later, she returned clandestinely to the bay,
picked up the three fugitives and slunk back out to sea. Thus was all
the blame passed to vanished individuals: there had been no
negligence on the part of any Valdivian official.

The colonel was having none of it, for he smelt a strong whiff of
collusion. If 'no direct neglect can be imputed to those in Command
at Valdivia', he wrote, acerbically, sceptically and by return, then the
escape could only be 'attributed to the very relaxed state of
Confinement in which those Prisoners were originally allowed to
exist'. To his repeated request that responsibility for allowing the
escape be better established, however, Secretary Tacornal parried with
an answer of great ingenuity. As Captain West, master of the *Ocean*,
was 'as I presume a subject of His Britannic Majesty and not now
being on the Chilian [sic] Territory', Tacornal requested that the
colonel, as His Majesty's nearest representative, would 'by the means

you possess, have condign punishment imposed for the offence' on Captain West and 'compel him to restore the Individuals carried away'.

This was a fatuous suggestion, a holding tactic rather than a real request, and both sides knew it: if representatives of foreign powers were allowed to inflict punishment on their own citizens on Chilean territory, the authority of the Chilean state would be unacceptably compromised. However, Secretary Tacornal's next paragraph was even worse. The colonel was assured that new orders had been issued for the remaining seven to be 'kept in due security', but Tacornal nevertheless thought it 'just to indicate to you that the measures restrictive of their liberty on mere presumption of Crime cannot be prolonged indefinitely, and that the Period is not very distant when the Government may find itself under the necessity of concluding it'.

Had they known of this latest letter of Tacornal's, the seven remaining men in Valdivia might have slept a little better. They did not: what they did know, however, was that even though HMS *Blonde* had been prevented from entering, she, or another British ship, would be back. If the British Consul-General knew who they were, and Commodore Mason knew where, then, as soon as the diplomatic bag got there, so must London—and when London knew, it would exert too much pressure for the Chilean authorities to withstand. They were right in this depressing calculation. A letter from the British Foreign Office had, in fact, reached Colonel Walpole in Valparaiso just before Commodore Mason returned from Valdivia with news of failure. This assured the colonel of that department's intention 'to confer with the Lords of the Admiralty as to the best mode of conveying these Offenders to Van Diemen's Land in order to be tried for the offences with which they stand charged'. It was exactly what the men had feared.

Governor Arthur's spluttering despatch to the Colonial Office, announcing the escape of ten men from Macquarie Harbour and

denouncing the incompetence of Captain Taw, had been entrusted
to the first naval captain sailing from Hobart. It arrived in London
in July. Descriptions of the fugitives were published in the *Police
Gazette* and the *Hue and Cry* and circulated to port authorities.
When Colonel Walpole's letter to the Foreign Office came off a ship
from Rio two months later, the two departments compared
information and realised immediately that the ten who had left Van
Diemen's Land were the same ten who had arrived in Valdivia. It
was therefore 'desirable', wrote Lord Stanley to his brother-peer
Lord Palmerston across the street, that the *Hue and Cry* 'should be
forwarded to . . . Chili [sic] as early as possible, with directions to
keep those convicts in safe Custody until further orders', giving
Colonel Walpole the proof of crimes committed that Secretary
Tacornal had requested and strengthening his arm in his demand for
stricter custody.

Copies of this despatch were immediately forwarded over the
Chilean hills to Don Joaquín Tacornal in the capital, with a note in
which the colonel expressed his 'trust that all doubt of the justice of
their detention' would finally be removed by these documents which
gave 'complete confirmation of the account delivered by the Deserters
themselves'. Surely now, the colonel thought, the Chilean government
could have no excuse for not ordering the immediate secure detention
of the seven still in Valdivia 'until arrangements . . . can be made for
their conveyance back to Van Diemen's Land, their [sic] to undergo
their trial'. Slowly, inexorably, the machinery of British detention and
pursuit was being set in motion.

The six men still in Valdivia, and the one now back on Doña Inés's
ranch, did not know the details of the correspondence crossing the
oceans on their account, but the possibility of a capture by the
Admiralty was looming ever larger in their minds. Apprehension
grew sharply at the end of the year, when the capital Santiago recalled

their friend Don Fernando from the post of *intendente*. In his place came Don Isaac Thompson, a Chilean national of British descent, who inherited a government palace with a ferrety little Englishman in residence and the task of keeping his companions in sight until the Supreme Government had decided what to do with them.

James Porter's friendship with Doña Inés was cooling as the cider season ended; a remark of the town magistrate to whom he had taken Antonietta had made an impression: 'her cruel disposition', that official had claimed, 'was the cause of her husband's shooting himself'. Whether from fear, boredom or something else, Porter 'now thought that I had been a long time about from my first friend, Don Lopez, I came to a resolution to return, and made mention of my determination to the young widow who took me by the hand and used all the art she was mistress of to detain me a month or two longer'. Resisting her charms—although greatly moved by the tearful farewell given him by the 'cholers and slaves that tilled the ground'— Porter returned to town and the family of Don Lopez, 'the whole of them transported with joy at seeing me'.

All seven remaining men were summoned to the palace shortly after Porter's return from the country, to be introduced to the new man in charge and take their leave of the old. Don Fernando had no doubt, he said, that Santiago's answer to their petition would be favourable, when it arrived—although this might take some time, as information had recently come in that the overland courier had been detained by the Indians and there was 'no knowing for a certainty when he will be allowed to come away as it is their drinking season'. Warmly recommending the men to his successor in the meantime, he expressed the hope that Governor Thompson would 'pay every attention to them as I have done, by placing dependence in them, I let them go where they please they gave me their word they would not try to make their escape, nor have they attempted it, therefore I consider them worthy of being at large'. It was a remarkable comment, given the recent escape of three aboard the *Ocean*.

Their first Christmas in Chile was thus an uneasy one, spent wondering how much Don Isaac knew, what his orders from Santiago had been and if—or when—the British would enter the bay and come to get them. The weather was cheerless: cold winds and heavy rain which turned the streets of Valdivia into mudslides and dripped through the wooden roofs. The only good news was that Antonietta, the Indian slave girl, had fled Doña Inés's house, fearing ill-treatment now Porter was no longer there to protect her, and had taken refuge with the Lopez's. They had agreed to purchase and keep her and shortly afterwards, Porter 'had the satisfaction of seeing her married to a peon, a faller of timber, who earned a very comfortable living'. In the first week of February 1835, the rains lessened and two of the English carpenters were at work aboard another sloop on the river when they raised their heads to a nasty surprise: a uniformed British officer was observing them from the shore.

The tall young man with the fatigued appearance and the drooping moustache was Captain Robert Fitzroy, commander of HMS *Beagle,* who had just brought his ship up from Chiloé in 'thick weather' with Charles Darwin and his party aboard. Now the *Beagle* lay under the forts and Captain Fitzroy had come upriver to pay a courtesy visit on the governor and be told of the 'Englishmen [who] had arrived in his district a few months before we came, whose character and business he did not understand'. According to Don Isaac Thompson, 'all but one were industrious members of his community'. Nevertheless, 'rumours had reached his ears', Fitzroy wrote in his journal, 'of their having escaped from one of our convict settlements, at the other side of the Pacific, and he was inclined to believe the report'.

Don Isaac was being less than truthful. Reports of the men's escape from Van Diemen's Land were more than rumours, and he knew it: they were substantiated by the men's own confessions to Don Fernando and information received at the end of last year from the British Consul-General. Perhaps Charles Darwin's diary note on the 'runaway convicts', made the same day as Captain Fitzroy's, gives the clue: 'the fact of their being such notorious rogues appears to have weighed nothing in the Governor's opinion, in comparison with the advantage of having some good Workmen'.

Uncertain though Don Isaac's sympathies were, it was true that the supply of work in the river had not changed. As Darwin rather contemptuously observed, the new governor was as keen as the old on turning to personal advantage the boat-building skills of his guests. The two men observed by Captain Fitzroy had been employed by Don Isaac himself, although he did not confide as much to his disapproving British visitor, to construct a whaleboat for his personal use. Nor had the others been prevented from continuing their employment. Nevertheless, the escape aboard the *Ocean* had left its mark, for all seven had found themselves under more rigorous parole. They did not like it. The new regime confirmed the suspicions that Mr Barker had put into their minds when the *Ocean* was in the estuary: that the British were on their way and their Chilean hosts were only housing them now in order to hand them over later. In fact, the more they lived under them, the more the new governor's rules 'looked', said Porter, 'as much like Macquarie Harbour Discipline that we were determined the first slant of wind we got we would take French leave for it and sail clear'. However, when, on the watch for opportunity, James Porter took work fitting out a barque some miles downriver, he was dismayed to find two soldiers sent on board to watch him.

Charles Darwin was little interested in these grubby mechanics and their affairs. He was more concerned with getting together horses and guides for his first foray into the town's damp and thickly forested hinterland. Captain Fitzroy, an officer of the Royal Navy with certain obligations to the crown, turned the matter over a few times in his mind but, having 'no proof of their delinquency', did not 'deem myself authorised to ask [the *intendente*] to have them arrested and delivered up to me, in order that I might convey them to the senior British officer at Valparaiso'. He thus made no attempt to approach the whaleboat where the two men were at work but merely watched and noted. Had he known the use they would later make of the vessel they were building, he might have reconsidered.

Within three days of the arrival of the *Beagle*, Darwin and some of the senior officers had disappeared inland on their endless search for specimens and samples, laden with nets and bottles and drawing pads, to cross the hills and gaze down on *los llanos* beyond. They were away for a week. On 19 February, the party slept once more in the town and was woken the next morning by the sound and spasm of earthquake. It was the worst to hit the Valdivian coast in 60 years.

All around, the houses, Darwin wrote, 'were violently shaken, and the boards creaked and rattled together'. People emerged into the streets, half-dressed, bewildered, with children in their arms, clutching each other as the earth lurched and slid beneath them, all 'in the greatest alarm', crying out and praying. In the woods behind the town, Robert Fitzroy had been lying on the ground, resting, when the earth moved beneath him. 'The sensation,' the captain mused, 'was something like a ship in a gentle seaway.' Down in the estuary, where the tide was at its lowest ebb, water came sliding swiftly over the sands to the high-water mark, shimmered and trembled there for some seconds, and receded again to its proper level. Curious, complicated currents emerged in the harbour and twisted the vessels one way and then violently another against their anchor warps. Small craft put out with anxious skippers aboard to throw out extra cables but were snatched and tossed about by the forces invisibly at work beneath them.

Valdivia was shaken but the town of Concepcion was destroyed, 'the earth cracked in all directions, roads blocked up with fallen rocks, cliffs shattered to pieces on the sea coast, fish etc. left on the dry land'. Vice-Consul Rouse wrote ruefully to Colonel Walpole that evening. 'Every kind of property is buried in the ruins. The inhabitants are living in the open air and a meeting is in contemplation to discuss the propriety of abandoning the site of the city for the winter and effecting huts in the neighbouring plain. I myself, sitting on the ground within sight of the wreck of my house, address this to you on a piece of Paper picked up by accident.'

When the *Beagle* put in at Concepcion a couple of days later, Darwin was fascinated by the beds of dead mussels and limpets left by the earthquake, visible even above the high-water line. Only a few months ago, he had been riding in the High Andes among the fossilised remains of sea animals. The raw materials for future fossils now lay visible on the Talcahuano beach. For Darwin, it was a step on the road to the theory of evolution. For Captain Fitzroy, stubbornly creationist, it was proof of 'the universality of the deluge'. For the local people it was a disaster. James Porter did not mention it at all.

Townsfolk and seamen might be working around them to rebuild and secure their livelihoods, but Porter and the six other remaining ship thieves were more concerned by the increasing surveillance under which they lived and worked. The atmosphere in town was changing, the townsfolk taking their cue from the new governor who, though prepared to employ the foreigners, did not treat them with the same cordiality and favour of the old. Don Lopez remained sanguine, advising James Porter only 'to remain quiet for a time and no doubt things would go better than I anticipated'. Mr Barker, however, again took the changes more seriously. He said the time was coming when they would have to steal another vessel and disappear and the plan beginning to form in his agile brain was a neat one. The whaleboat on which the English carpenters were at work for Don Isaac would soon be completed. It was in this, rendered sturdy and well-provisioned for her maiden voyage, that 'they meant to make their escape', and it would be soon. Pressing upon him the need for discretion, Barker told Porter to 'hold myself in readiness'.

The four men planning to escape in the governor's whaleboat were Mr Barker, Bristol seaman James Lesley, carpenter Benjamin Russen and James Porter. Again, William Cheshire was not invited. Nor, this time, were Billy Shires and Charles Lyon to be of the party. John Barker was prepared to abandon his second wife but Billy Shires, now father of the baby Bernardo, had decided to risk staying put. Porter does not write of why Lyon was not included but with hindsight, and judging by the deterioration in their relationship much dwelt upon later in his narrative, it seems likely Lyon had already become unpopular with his mates, forming his own little clique with the other outsider, William Cheshire.

A year and three weeks after their arrival in the bay of Valdivia, Mr Barker told Porter that the escape was planned for the following Sunday. The other three would collect him from his lodgings en route to the whaleboat and they would make away downriver in the dark, sneak below the forts and be gone by morning. On Saturday night, Porter 'turned into my Bunk in expectation of it being the last night'. It was not to be. For the third time in two years, his awakening was to boots planted either side of his head and the barrel of a musket in his face. In the *cuartel*, he found William Cheshire and Charles Lyon fastened back to back and Billy Shires with one of a pair of irons around his wrists and ankles, the other waiting for the hands and legs of James Porter. Barker, Lesley and Russen had bolted the day before, the alarm had been given and orders sent out to round up the remaining four. James Porter had been betrayed. If he knew or suspected the reason, he did not give it in his memoirs.

Under the eye of the gaol guard, he was desolate. 'I then,' he would write, 'give up all hopes of ever regaining my liberty.'

9

The Persistence of Colonel Walpole

When news came from Don Joaquín Tacornal of a second successful escape from Valdivia, and one aboard a boat belonging to the governor himself, Colonel Walpole's anger was scarcely containable.

'Compelled by a sense of duty,' he wrote, '*again* to call the attention of the Chilian [sic] Government to the conduct of the authorities at Valdivia in regard to the British Prisoners confined in that Fortress,' it was, he reminded them, 'originally the desire and intention of the Chilian Government to retain those Prisoners in such a state of Confinement as might as found to conciliate the security of their Persons with the dictates of Humanity.' He was therefore 'disappointed' (surely he toyed with a stronger word) to have 'received official information that the Governor had employed those Prisoners in a work, by the means of which when completed three of them were enabled to and have, as might from former experience have been foretold, made their escape. "Unwilling" though "the Undersigned" was, he continued to doubt the sincerity of the professions made by the Chilian [sic] Government on this subject, he cannot but consider this proceeding of the Governor as a culpable remissness in the execution of the directions forwarded to him, and he has therefore to request that, should the statement received prove on enquiry to be correct, some unequivocal mark of the displeasure of the Chilian Government may be furnished to him for the satisfaction of His Britannic Majesty's Government.'

Colonel Walpole's language was strong but any hopes that his request would be met by action were faint: after a year's hedging and stalling, the colonel had dismissed his Chilean partners as suffering from an 'almost insuperable antipathy to severity of any kind'. Secretary Tacornal's reply did nothing to change this opinion. There was no apology and little explanation; merely a feeble attempt to defend his subordinate. The men had escaped 'before the orders which were given on the subject to the Governor of Valdivia in consequence of the Information received from you' arrived and 'even before he received the Instructions . . . which were sent by the [overland] post'. Given that Tacornal had learnt of the presence and probable identity of the men over a year ago, the fact that his instructions to hold them in safe custody were so late was little excuse. He promised that Don Isaac would be 'seriously expostulated with' about this 'disagreeable Event' and assured the British consul that a second Valdivian enquiry would be held to ascertain the circumstances of this latest Valdivian escape. The colonel was not impressed by the promises.

Don Isaac's people in Valdivia did not rush their enquiry— unsurprisingly, as the governor's naivety must feature embarrassingly in any conclusion, as well as the dilatory fashion in which he had executed his duties. It had taken an entire month before he got around to sending a letter to the governor of neighbouring Concepcion province, 'through which the *intendente* of Valdivia presumes [the men] will pass', informing him that 'three individuals deserters from Van Diemen's Land, had broken prison'. The capture of these individuals, he continued fatuously, was 'recommended very expressly in order not to counteract the zeal and punctuality with which he desired to fulfil the wishes of the Government from whom he received orders to keep them in security until the question should be decided whether they had a claim to the Right of Asylum'. Descriptions of John Barker, Benjamin Russen and James Lesley were enclosed but the authorities in Concepcion, unaware of the escape and in any case immersed in the massive work of reconstruction after the earthquake, had taken no notice of three Englishmen who arrived quietly at the end of March, ditched their whaleboat and headed inland.

What did change abruptly after this second escape were the conditions in which those left behind were held. All parole rescinded, they were kept in the *cuartel* which had originally hosted them on their arrival just over a year ago. While higher powers argued the details of their status and their future, the four disputed men would, at last, be held in the 'safe Custody' that Colonel Walpole had been demanding. Don Isaac had learnt his lesson, late but well.

Their incarceration in the *cuartel* might have been cut short but for a second disastrous event on the coast above Valdivia. In April, HMS *Challenger* had left Rio for Valparaiso under the command of Captain Michael Seymour. She rounded the Horn in high seas at the end of that month and turned northwards up the Araucanian coast. Captain Seymour could not take sights in the poor weather but his deduced reckoning put her a good 60 miles off the coast by noon on 19 May 1835. Late that night, thick rain had turned the air to a salty soup and reduced visibility to almost nothing when the lookout's panicky yells brought the captain and first mate flying on deck. They were too late: within minutes, the *Challenger* had run aground at the mouth of the river Leubu and by dawn the Araucanians were gathering.

It took almost a month before news of the shipwreck reached Valparaiso. The people of Concepcion, their town in ruins around them, had been able to extend little help to the Englishmen and they were still camped in the Leubu estuary, scared, short of food, some of them sick. It was the worst possible weather to mount a rescue, for wild winds blowing directly onshore made the Leubu river mouth almost inaccessible: any ship going to the rescue of the *Challenger*'s passengers risked being blown ashore and joining them if she were not managed with exemplary seamanship. It was Captain Fitzroy who insisted they must nevertheless go immediately, Commodore Mason hesitating to such an extent that very sharp words were exchanged and Fitzroy was even heard to mutter about court martial. When the *Blonde* hove-to off the coast where Seymour's men were camped, it was again Robert Fitzroy who acted as pilot and forced the mission through, eventually managing to bring away all 70 exhausted men. A letter from Fitzroy to Captain Seymour's later court martial persuaded his judges that his error in deduced reckoning had been due not to incompetence but to the alteration in the coastal currents brought about by the recent earthquake, of which Seymour, having only just come round the Horn, knew nothing. He was honourably absolved.

With the loss of the *Challenger* and the upheaval of earthquake, it was not until the beginning of September that Colonel Walpole learnt that another royal frigate would soon be in the area. Wondering what further evasions and obfuscations were in store, he gritted his teeth and wrote to Secretary Tacornal, 'conced[ing] himself the Honor ... to request His Excellency to furnish him with the requisite order and directions to the Governor of Valdivia for the safe delivery of the remaining Prisoners into the hands of the Officer in Command of the Vessel'. As he had feared, Tacornal did not oblige. Instead of sending the documents requested, he asked Colonel Walpole to attend his offices to discuss the case.

A long conference at the Ministry for Foreign Affairs in Santiago began with Tacornal's assurances that 'the Chilian [sic] Government were anxious to give every proof of its desire to act on every occasion in such a mode as should manifest to the British government the sincere friendship which it was anxious to maintain with it'. Chile was, nevertheless, reluctant to deliver the men up: no longer because there was any lack of information about their provenance but, rather, because of misgivings aroused by a sentence in Colonel Walpole's earlier correspondence. Back on 25 April, the colonel had stated that the men's seizure of the *Frederick* had 'add[ed] to the Catalogue of those [crimes] for which they were lawfully undergoing Punishment the atrocious Crime of Piracy' and it was because piracy carried an automatic death sentence that Tacornal now found himself unable to hand the men over. Although their acts, he explained, 'might be considered as amounting to Piracy according to the British statutes', nevertheless 'it was difficult to construe [them] as such according to the definition given to that term by Writers on International Law' and thus they 'could not be classed in that list of Crimes of which the Perpetrators were by universal agreement delivered up by one friendly Nation at the request of another'.

'It is unnecessary for me,' wrote a weary colonel to Lord Palmerston the following day, 'to trouble your Lordship with the details of the long conversation which ensued.' It had been a tiring, tendentious discussion. The position of the Chilean government was this: that the ship thieves had not committed piracy, because they had seized the vessel 'solely for the purpose of effecting their Escape', not 'with a view to profitable plunder'. The colonel's rejoinder was that firstly, the Chilean government were wrong to draw this conclusion from the works of international law on which they had based it; and, secondly, that even had their conclusion been correct, overpowering a crew and making away with a vessel—piracy or not—could never be justified when its objective was to escape a legally authorised punishment, in this case a sentence of transportation. Don Joaquín had offered a cigar: could the colonel persuade him he was in the legal right, of course he would be delighted to give the criminals up, but the colonel must understand his position . . . Latinisms were tossed about and cups of coffee drunk. The colonel sweated. Tacornal remained sleek in the heat and protested his government's earnest desire to remain on good terms with Britain. Baited beyond endurance, the colonel left.

Two weeks later, Colonel Walpole received utterly unexpected news of capitulation. A letter from Tacornal, although reiterating the 'difficulties which the government of Chile have met with in considering those individuals as real Pirates—understanding that expression not according to the particular acceptation given to it by the statutes of some nations but according to that given to it by the Law of Nations'—a disagreeable slur on the precision of British law—nevertheless conceded that 'you require them in the name of the British government as *Pirates*, and the Government of Chile has decided to deliver them up to you as such'. Then came another swipe. The Chilean government was . . .

> induced to hope that if when tried by the competent Tribunal they should not be pronounced guilty of Piracy in the abovementioned sense, they may be permitted to enjoy the benefit of that asylum which they will be able to procure in a foreign land and of which the Government of Chile would not have deprived them if not for the opinion so positively and repeatedly expressed by yourself that they have been guilty of that crime, constituted themselves enemies of the Human Race and unworthy of the Protection of the Law of Nations.

The President would have considered himself as failing in the duty of humanity (and the fallen state of the culprits would not render this impression less painful to him) if he did not express this hope to you in the firm conviction that it will be favourably received by the rectitude and humanity of the British Government.

The colonel may have bristled at this rebuke but he had got what he wanted and returned a gracious reply, asking to be informed of the expenses run up by the men during their stay in Valdivia 'in order that the same may be immediately liquidated'. His persistence was finally paying off: six were gone but four were in custody, the Chilean government had conceded the argument and all that was wanted was a ship to bring the men away.

In Concepcion, at the end of a year dominated by earthquake and shipwreck, Vice-Consul Rouse also received a piece of good news. On 23 December, Benjamin Russen and James Lesley had been arrested while drinking in a local bar, nine months after they had fled Valdivia aboard Governor Thompson's whaleboat. They were being held in the town gaol when the governor of Concepcion summoned Vice-Consul Rouse to interpret. That evening, the men were brought in, 'examined one by one' and 'minutely interrogated as to the slightest incident which might contribute to the discovery of the convicts who were sought for'. The descriptions belatedly sent up from Valdivia were located and, in Mr Rouse's presence, the men were examined and were found to 'coincide exactly with the marks in the descriptions': the mark beneath James Lesley's eyebrow, his grey eyes and high temples; the anchor tattoo on Benjamin Russen's right arm and the scars on his nose, cheek and upper lip. Governor Boza of Concepcion sent the two men back to gaol while he requested orders from Santiago. On Christmas Day, the Chilean brig *Orion* entered the harbour en route for Valparaiso and Governor Boza announced his intention of putting the Englishmen on board.

Five days later, the brig had sailed without them and James Lesley had bribed the sergeant of the gaol guard and escaped.

The temporary rapprochement brought about by Secretary Tacornal's capitulation over the definition of piracy was over. This latest Chilean laxity called forth the strongest reproof and the clearest expression of contempt yet made.

Colonel Walpole, his pen almost tearing through the paper, wrote the following:

> The Undersigned has already so repeatedly and ineffectually called on the Chilian [sic] government for a practical proof of its disapprobation of such laxity of Vigilance exercised by those immediately placed as Guard over these Prisoners that he will here refrain from any further similar demand and he will limit himself to drawing the attention of the Chilian government to the unfavourable impression which must inevitably be caused on other governments when they observe that however in accordance with the generally-recognised principles may be the Chilian government, in questions of a friendly nature arising between them, in its Power to carry them into effect it appears to be essentially deficient.

Tacornal wrote to the President, the President wrote to Concepcion and Governor Boza of that town set afoot an enquiry. The colonel was assured that everything was being done to ascertain the circumstances of this unfortunate case and to bring back the man who had escaped. While the enquiry was sitting, Benjamin Russen, too, went over the prison wall and disappeared into the night.

Governor Boza's report into the circumstances of the two escapes, when it eventually came some months later, was a masterpiece: measures had been adopted and requisitions had been expedited; interrogations had been minute and searches thorough. Nonetheless, it appeared that no one was at fault and nothing could have been prevented.

Answers to awkward questions were buried in long, long sentences. Why were the men not fettered after the December interrogation yielded strong suspicions of their identity? Because 'the orders requiring them to be seized enforced no more than their simple detention'. No one had mentioned fetters. Why had they not been put aboard the brig for Valparaiso and British custody? 'Taking into consideration that neither the declarations which had been taken . . . nor the comparison of the description marks formed a legal certainty of their really being fugitives from Van Diemen's Land', Governor Boza had 'suspended preparations for their departure'. But did the governor not earlier find that the men 'coincided exactly with the marks in the descriptions?' Yes, but 'the recommendation of the apprehension and detention of the foreigners from the Intendant of Valdivia' did not specifically 'direct that they should be sent to [Valparaiso]'. Could he not at least have sent word to Valparaiso or Valdivia of the arrest of wanted men? He had, indeed, considered doing so but 'afterwards I did not think it necessary to do so much because this affair had not been entrusted to this intendency directly by the Ministry'; and, presuming a copy of Governor Isaac Thompson's letter announcing the men's earlier escape from Valdivia had been sent to the Governor of Valparaiso, 'it was very probable that the Governor of Valparaiso to whom the order was given to seize the English fugitives would announce the result of their seizure'. It did not actually, strictly, fall to him to tell that governor of their arrest in order to facilitate this announcement.

As to any culpability among the officers of the Concepcion gaol: the trial of the sergeant bribed by James Lesley was 'pending in the military court'. The 'most diligent enquiries' were being made into the escape of Benjamin Russen 'to render clear and to question the culpability which the individuals of the Guard over the prison might have incurred'. Finally, why had not Mr Rouse's offer of a reward for the men's apprehension been accepted? 'The interest which this Intendancy took in the affair,' explained Governor Boza enigmatically—or perhaps not—'caused it to refuse the admission of this offer.'

When a copy of this report was forwarded to Colonel Walpole, he did not even send an acknowledgement.

Permission from the Chilean government for British naval officers to take custody of the four men left in the gaol of Valdivia had been granted in September, but all this prevarication and enquiry and explanation meant that much time had gone by before news of Santiago's capitulation reached Valdivia. 'We had been about seven months chained together like Dogs,' James Porter wrote, when the faithful Don Lopez told him of the gossip that 'a vessel belonging to the English' was on its way. 'This,' he continued, 'touched me to the quick and I was determined to make a bold finish for it.'

If any escape attempt were to be made, he must first free himself of Billy Shires and then of his irons. The first was accomplished by persuading Shires to 'complain of sickness, so we should be separated'. In place of the chains, the gaolers fitted Porter with a pair of bar irons 'the Bar coming across my instep so that I could only walk about 4 inches at a step'. Thus hobbled, another seven weeks went past while he waited for opportunity. It came with the slave girl Antonietta, who 'came in to see me, and cryed very much I begged of her not to cry but asked her if I could trust her with a secret'. Seeing her 'dark eyes sparkle' once again, he told her to 'go immediately and bring me a thin knife and file, and do not let a soul know what you are going to do'. Doubts assailed him over the unwisdom of trusting females with secrets (although when the time came to write his memoirs, he had concluded they were 'true and staunch as my own sex'). Sure enough, back she came with a file 'secreted in her long black hair' and a knife 'up the sleeve of her gown' and 'with a pitiful countenance ejaculated, Santa Maria protect you!'

That evening, Porter notched the knife with the file and sawed through the bar. He would go at eight, the hour at which the guard was changed. A few minutes before the bell rang, he got up from the fireside, where he had been sitting chatting with his fellow prisoners and a group of soldiers, and hobbled towards the door which led to the backyard and the privies, secretly squeezing Shires' hand as he went by. He told the sentinel he had the sergeant's leave and the man let him pass. Immediately, he shook off the irons, placed a plank against the high wall of the yard, ran up it, barefoot, to catch the top of the wall and haul himself over and saw the door open behind him as he went.

News of the latest escape from the *cuartel* quickly went round town. Some were on the side of Governor Isaac Thompson, wishing they could rid themselves of these pesky foreigners so they could become someone else's problem. Others were sympathetic to the men's cause: young ones like Antonietta, who knew the men personally and wished to help them; employers, friends of their wives and their wives' families; those who had heard tales of the suffering in Van Diemen's Land and thought they should not be handed back to the inflexible British. Porter was out in the South American interior for longer than he had ever managed in Van Diemen's Land and they were seven days of flight, theft and struggle. When the soldiers caught up with him, huddled under a poncho stolen at knifepoint, wretchedly sick with dysentery, they tied his feet together under the belly of a horse and brought him back to Valdivia. There, they took him to the blacksmith's shop and he was 'ordered to stand upon a large anvil' where the irons were put on 'and a piece of iron [red hot] lifted hissing from the fire was placed in the end of the bar and actually welded in'.

This humiliation was deliberately public but excited as much comment against Governor Thompson as against the foreign fugitive. There were 'many young people', Porter wrote, 'both male and female pitying me and many among them crying expecting I should be shot in the morning with the irons on me'. Half-dead already from fatigue, exposure and beating, he did not much care whether he were or not. When several townspeople came to the gaol that night to offer him comfort and hope, he told them he 'was quite resigned to my fate'. But the following morning, the expected guard did not come at six to take him away and blindfold him against the bullets. Instead, a priest came into the cell with news. He and a group of 'females of distinction' had spent much of the night prevailing upon Governor Thompson to spare the Englishman's life and the governor had, after much argument, consented. Perhaps the pleading ladies and the men of the cloth did persuade Thompson to clemency; more likely the threatened death sentence had been no more than a piece of spite. Executing a British subject for the offence of absconding while awaiting collection by the British authorities would be looked upon unfavourably in London. Governor Thompson, already smarting under reprimands from Santiago, could not afford to blot his copybook again.

With one man welded into his irons and the other three cowed into submission by darkness, discomfort and malnutrition, the remaining ship thieves were abruptly plucked from the cells one afternoon in late April 1836, when the town was siesta-quiet, and escorted to the bay. There, an ensign flew brightly from HMS *Basilisk,* at anchor under the forts. The next morning, James Porter, Charles Lyon, William Shires and William Cheshire left Valdivia forever.

The officers of the *Basilisk* treated the four 'with humane kindness, pitying our unfortunate situation'. Two of the sailors aboard were old acquaintances of James Porter and, 'a sailor's heart always being open to a shipmate in distress, they relieved me in every sense of the word'. Nevertheless, the irons that held all four of them to the same bar stayed put throughout the week they spent detained in the gunroom. On 7 May, the *Basilisk* was in Valparaiso and the young lieutenant in command wrote a brief note to Colonel Walpole.

> We arrived today from Valdivia, where we were sent by Commodore Mason and received on board the 4 men named in margin (James Porter, William Shires, William Cheshire, Charles Lyons), with 2 sets of irons for which I gave a receipt and victualled on board at 2/3 the allowance of a seaman but without spirits.

His mission accomplished, the lieutenant handed the men over to his commodore aboard the *Blonde,* which set off immediately for Callao. When she pulled into some small port en route, James Porter made his last attempt at South American freedom.

His plan was the most primitive yet: to break his irons, jump over the side and swim for it. The difficulty was that if one man were to break free from the bar to which all were chained, the rest had to be told of the plan. All four agreed to try and, as Billy Shires could not swim, the other three promised they would support him to the shore. In the afternoon, three were released from the bar to go forward, escorted, to the heads while Porter managed to 'oval the shackles'. When they came back, William Shires had reconsidered his participation.

> I should be sorry to be the means of being a check on your liberty, Jimmy, [he said], I care not for the other two we know they are scoundrels . . . when I am overboard they may desert us, and I should be too heavy for you which may be the means of your being taken and

them two get clear off. I will stop behind it will be far better for me to die an ignominious death than the both of us, my only request is, that should you get clear off, you will not forget to see Catalina my wife, also my little Boy, and be a friend to them.

By ill-fortune, it was a cloudless, moonlit night when Porter woke first Lyon then Cheshire, and found both had changed their minds. He would not change his. Placing his jacket on the bed 'to make it appear should the sentinel look over that I was sleeping with my head under the clothes', he went. It was a forlorn attempt: he had scarcely reached the mizzen chains when a pistol was put to his head with a marine behind it. Later, it was whispered in his ear by a sailor that the marines had been alerted by Lyons and Cheshire, shaking their chains.

When the first lieutenant called Porter to explain himself, the fatigue of too much time in irons was heavy in his words.

> I informed him I thought I had been prisoner long enough and knowing myself innocent of any crime I considered I had an undoubted right to escape if I could, and that he could give orders to the sentinel that if he saw me away from the Guns where I was confined to shoot me, and by the same rule if I saw the sentinel off his guard I would go overboard in spite of fate let the consequence be what it would.

It was brave and defiant and the officers did not punish him, for Commodore Mason himself said 'it is natural the man would try to make his escape—if they are guilty of the crime they are charged with, they are to be pitied, and if no, then the case is very aggravating to them'; but their irons were secured more tightly and no further opportunity came to test the sentinel's aim.

At Callao, the men were transhipped to the *North Star* to battle through the icebergs, round the Horn and make a rough passage home. By late October, they were aboard the *Leviathan*, a prison-hulk in Portsmouth harbour, awaiting the next transport-ship to Australia. There, they 'went through a thorough repair, clean washed, and close shaved' and were given 'the riggins' of a convict. They were back in the government cloth.

In Valdivia, wives, girlfriends, babies and friends waited for news that would never come.

10

The Voyage of the Sarah

*I*t had been a nine-year absence from Britain for William Cheshire, twelve years for James Porter and Charles Lyon, and twenty-six for Billy Shires, transported for life when he was still in his teens. Britain had changed. Fat King George had died of his vices and ceded the throne to his brother King William IV, who would soon pass it on to his teenage niece, Victoria. Intense popular pressure had produced the Reform Act of 1832, which emancipated several thousand males to preserve the status quo. Demand from below had forced the reformed House of Commons to outlaw slavery in all British colonies. Now Lord John Russell, Home Secretary of a Whig government, drafter of the 1832 act, young and determined, had grand plans to extend reform to the criminal law, reduce the number of crimes to which his predecessors had extended the death penalty and abolish the centuries-old practice of penal transportation.

Just like the sugar-slaves in Demerara and Barbados, the old lags breaking rock in the Australian road gangs would have laughed had they been told of the passion for abolition that had animated Britain in recent years. Anti-slavery societies had been petitioning Parliament for decades and legislation and judicial decisions had been slowly but inexorably working towards the abolitionist dream. First it was confirmed that the status of slave could not exist on British soil; then the slave trade to British possessions overseas was outlawed, although slavery was allowed to continue where it had already been established; then the agreements with other slave-owning powers began to be made and enforced and the Royal Navy went out to patrol the slavers' ways. Now, it remained only to force Parliament to outlaw slavery throughout the British empire overseas and free the 'Negro brother' from the plantations. The conditions of West Indian slavery were brought continually before the British public: floggings and mutilations, harsh labour, spiked collars, degradation and despair; the sending of pregnant women to the treadmill; the 'disobedient' girls whose masters raped them, shaved their heads and whipped them until they miscarried. Eventually the parliamentary debate began and led to an act in 1833 that abolished slavery in all British territories. Now, Lord John Russell and his allies in the cabinet were turning their attention to transportation, a punishment which they considered as archaic as hanging for the theft of a pheasant.

As yet, the anti-transportation movement was young and many saw nothing wrong in the old system. Another year and a half would elapse before the establishment of the parliamentary committee that would condemn transportation to death, using a report written by its chairman, Sir William Molesworth, with the backing of Lord John Russell. This mighty and damning work would, as Russell knew when he commissioned Molesworth to research it, yield the factual ammunition to persuade Parliament to abolish transportation as it had abolished slavery. Until the Molesworth committee presented its conclusions in three years' time, the system would continue at both ends of the world with few substantial changes to the mechanisms established in 1788: gaol delivery, hulk and transportation followed by assignment, emancipation and respectability; or by descent, hard labour and degradation. When the *North Star* came into Portsmouth in October 1836 with four desolate Britons chained on the gundeck, thirteen convict ships had already left for Australia since the beginning of that year. Three more would follow, bringing the year's tally of transported felons to 3943. Of these, 1655 went to the increasingly crowded island of Van Diemen's Land and the rest to the larger spaces of New South Wales and what would become Victoria.

One of the Admiralty's transport commissions was riding to anchor just outside Portsmouth harbour when the *North Star* arrived. She was HM Convict Ship *Sarah*, a 480-ton London brig converted from commercial to penal use, intended to leave for Van Diemen's Land in early November and slowly taking on her convict cargo. Inside the breakwater, the four ship thieves from Valdivia were moved from the *Leviathan* to the *Britannia* guard ship to be watched over by marines. With Portsmouth town within swimming distance, Porter and his mates were more closely guarded than they had been at sea: 'handcuffed, two by two, upon two gratings', wrote Porter indignantly, 'with four Marines over us and a man for the express purpose of cutting our provisions up in small pieces when we had to convey it to our mouths the best way we could . . . we were not even allowed to go to the head without a lump of a Marine being lashed to each of us'. On the docks they could see but not reach, 254 male felons were being offloaded from prison-cart and wagon, brought from gaols all over England to stand dismally on the quays, be stared at by the crowds and await their turn in the lighters which took them out to their new prison on the water.

James McTernan, royal naval surgeon, had just taken up his position as surgeon-superintendent aboard the *Sarah*. It would be his fifth voyage to Australia aboard a prison-ship. The position of surgeon-superintendent had been introduced when the last official report into the transportation system, delivered in 1822, exposed the dishonesty of officers previously entrusted with convict care: holding back rations, sexual abuse, selling government property for private gain. The welfare of the convicts was the surgeon-superintendent's direct responsibility. Entitled to 'half a guinea per head for every prisoner he delivers safe and sound at the end of the voyage, on receiving a certificate from the Governor of that colony that his conduct has merited such a gratuity', he had 'every inducement', as one gentleman convict had observed, 'to exercise the greatest attention and vigilance, and to see that everyone receives his just allowance'.

Studying names, offences and sentences in the *Sarah*'s Transportation Register, Dr McTernan found, as he expected, that most of those aboard were thieves, burglars, muggers, pickpockets, fraudsters and forgers—men from the same spectral 'criminal class' that British Crown and Circuit judges had been weeding, thinning, pruning and sending to 'Parts Beyond the Seas' for centuries: first the East and West Indies, then America and Canada and finally, when the North Americans no longer wanted them, to Australia. There were, however, some disturbing additions to the familiar list of louts and unfortunates aboard the *Sarah*. Forty-nine of the men now awaiting departure in berths at the bottom of the ship had been sentenced by courts martial sitting thousands of miles away from England. Some of these had been keeping the *Pax Britannica* in Nova Scotia, Quebec and Ontario, Newfoundland, Gibraltar, Grenada and Montserrat. Others had been on duty guarding the precious sugar islands of the West Indies: Barbados, Grenada, Trinidad and Jamaica. All had fallen foul of regimental discipline, disobeyed their officers, deserted or gone drinking, thieving and raping. They were not the first ex-servicemen to sail in chains for Australia, for military felons were subject to this punishment no less than civilian ones, but it was unusual for any one ship to carry so large a group of former soldiers.

Even more unusual was a group of 22 men identified by odd-sounding names in the Register: 'Hamlet', 'Billy', 'Blue Boy'. These men represented another side of British colonial life. From the occupations ascribed them in the Convict Muster, they appear little different to the other convicts: Billy had been a 'carter and bullock driver' in Barbados before being sentenced for burglary; Hamlet an 'indoor servant and groom' who turned to housebreaking; Blue Boy a 'gentleman's servant and groom' before he stole a mare. In fact, they were all former slaves and their presence on board a transportation ship, sailing into penal servitude, was an indirect consequence of their release from slavery.

When news had arrived in the West Indies that the British parliament planned to abolish slavery, masters were enraged and slaves were jubilant. They jumped the gun, rose, celebrated liberty prematurely and were beaten back by British regiments and gun-toting plantocrats. When abolition finally did come into force, on 1 August 1834, the slave islands were in the anarchic and bloody aftermath of revolt: white magistrates saw insurrection lurking behind every black felony or misdemeanour. Where these had previously met with sentences of flogging or imprisonment, it was now punished with transportation to Australia. Between 1831 and 1838, one hundred and forty black felons were despatched to travel the globe in various floating prisons: the frigates of the Caribbean station to Britain; then hulks in the Thames or the Solent; finally convict-ships to Australia. Men enslaved for generations, free for twelve or 24 months, found themselves once again in shackles with the new status of transported felon.

Aboard the *Sarah*, the result was an uneasy, volatile mix. Black men who despaired of ever seeing their homes, sick from the cold,

The ship thieves planned to round New Zealand, go north until that country was out of sight, then sail east along the parallel until they hit America, or America hit them. It was a dangerous journey and it was necessary to stay alert. As these two images depict, thousands of mariners drowned doing exactly what those aboard the *Frederick* were trying to do.

ATLANTIC

EUROPE

ASIA

AFRICA

INDIAN OCEAN

AUSTRALIA

TASMANI

The Voyages
of
Convict James Porter

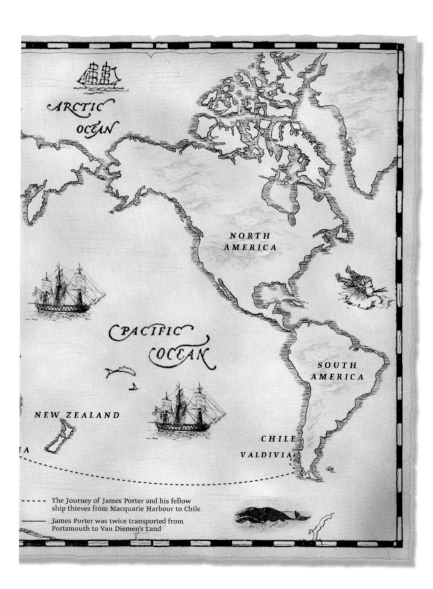

ARCTIC
OCEAN

NORTH
AMERICA

PACIFIC
OCEAN

SOUTH
AMERICA

NEW ZEALAND

CHILE
VALDIVIA

- - - - The Journey of James Porter and his fellow
ship thieves from Macquarie Harbour to Chile

———— James Porter was twice transported from
Portsmouth to Van Diemen's Land

After covering 6000 miles through gales and rough seas the *Frederick* reached the Chilean coast. The ship thieves had spent six weeks and a day onboard. But their destination of Valparaiso Harbour *(above)* was seemingly still out of reach.

News of the ship thieves' presence and identity quickly spread throughout Valdivia. Word would eventually find its way to the inhabitants of Concepcion, where the nearest British vice-consulate was located.

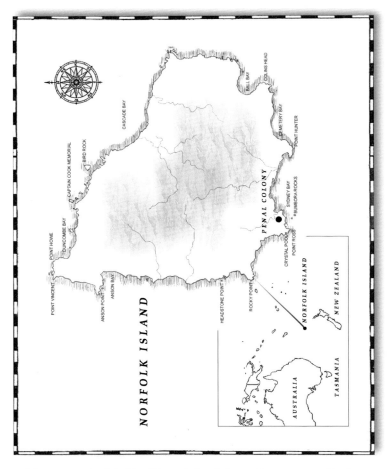

After arriving back in Van Diemen's Land, James Porter appeared before Chief Justice Pedder and a jury of ten soldiers in the Hobart courtroom. The verdict would see him bound for Norfolk Island – his fourth voyage in chains.

If Porter thought Hell's Gates in Macquarie Harbour was frightening, the waters around Norfolk Island were equally dangerous – and the place even more difficult to escape from.

On 26th August 1839, in cold midwinter weather, Porter arrived at Norfolk Island. The conditions he found there were the worst yet encountered in a lifetime of gaols and labour camps.

Backs, and at this time they were getting 131

~~Porter~~, at this time ²³ I got pen ink and paper with a
view to write a letter to my friends and while meditating
upon my truly unfortunate situation those few
lines came into my head —

How wretched is an Exile's state of mind
When not one gleam of hope on earth remain
Though grief worn down, with servile chains confined;
And not one friend to sooth his heartfelt pain.

Too true I know that man was made to mourn
A heavy portion's fallen to my lot
With anguish full my aching heart is torn
Far from my friends by all the world forgot,

The feathered race with splendid plumage gay
Extend their throats with a discordant sound
With Liberty they spring from spray to spray
While I a wretched Exile gaze around

Farewell my Sister, Aged Parents dear,
Ere long my glass of life will cease to run
In silence drop a sympathetic tear
For your Unhappy: Exiled: long lost Son;

O Cease my troubled aching heart to beat
Since happiness so far from thee has fled
Haste, haste unto your silent cold retreat
In clay cold earth to mingle with the Dead

  I had scarcely finished it; when a Soldier

While on Norfolk Island, Porter expanded on the brief memoir he had written
while in Hobart gaol. His writing included poetry. Here he writes of the
wretched life of an exiled convict. The poem is quoted on pages 166–67.

SYDNEY COVE.

In May 1843, James Porter left Norfolk Island, the Island of Demons, and, 'much worn out but steady and well conducted', arrived in Sydney Cove. In that busy and prosperous city James Porter was heard from no more.

unable to communicate with those around them, lay in the narrow berths and close air of the orlop deck beside some of the white soldiers who had brutally and unquestioningly ruled them.

Just before the ship was due to sail, four more men were bundled aboard with a letter for Dr McTernan, as Colonial Secretary Lord Glenelg considered them sufficiently dangerous to bring their presence to his particular notice. 'Among those put under my charge,' wrote Dr McTernan, 'were four "escaped Convicts" regarding whose capture of the Colonial brig "Frederick" under circumstances of great atrocity, I had received due notification for my guidance.' Tales of the hijack in Macquarie Harbour must have been embroidered, for the men had, in fact, taken pains not to commit atrocity in their treatment of those put ashore. Perhaps Dr McTernan assumed that mutiny and atrocity went perforce together; what was not mere assumption was that these men were returning to a certain capital sentence and had every reason for desperate action.

There were too many men experienced in violence aboard the *Sarah*, and Dr McTernan had been on his guard from the moment he took up his duty and scanned the Transportation Register. He was no more cautious than any other of his rank, for the officer of the 1830s surveyed a scene where mutiny was to be expected, and, if not harshly and immediately suppressed, would lead to dreadful consequences.

Dr McTernan had first shepherded convicts to Sydney in 1823. On that voyage, five days out from Portsmouth, two convict informers had come forward separately and named five ringleaders who, they said, were plotting mutiny. McTernan suppressed the rising, the leaders were flogged and the other suspects kept in irons. The *Isabella*, sailing the same route that year under another surgeon-superintendent, reported an identical pattern of events; so did the *Mangles*, in 1824, and the *Royal Charlotte*, of 1825, and ship after ship during the next decade. While surgeon-superintendents relied on convict informers from the orlop, captains were wise to keep a close eye on mutterings among the seamen in the fo'c'sle. In these years of emigration boom, only those who could not find better work took up a contract to take a gang of convicts to the bottom of the world. Seamen on transport ships were, on the whole, a brutish and untrustworthy lot, susceptible to incitement and, although their grievances did not always overlap with those of the convicts, the possibility of their joining forces aboard an unhappy ship kept officers awake in the small hours. Four years ago, two crews had rebelled, refusing duty and breaking into the liquor. Many other ships had arrived in Sydney or Hobart one man down, not because of accident or illness, but because he was in irons somewhere below deck.

On the *Sarah*, Dr McTernan and his fellow officers had more reason than most to suspect that rebellion might be planned: 49 old soldiers— one-fifth of the men crammed onto the orlop deck—of whom fourteen were lifers with little to lose; 21 men from the islands where slaves had recently turned on their masters; and a gang of desperate mutineers sent aboard at the last moment—it did not bode well.

December came and the *Sarah* was still anchored off Spithead with her full complement of convicts aboard. She had been due to sail on 29 November and Dr McTernan, writing 'in momentary expectation of his sailing orders', had hoped to be in Hobart Town by the end of February. But the winter winds came howling across the water from Newfoundland: thick, westerly gales full of Atlantic rain which swung the *Sarah* dangerously about, made the anchor cable stretch and groan and persuaded Captain Whiteside that she must return to the shelter of Portsmouth harbour until they passed. The harbour, with scores of vessels crammed together waiting out the gales, was a furious din of halyard against mast and wet wind through the rigging. The convict-ship *George* was anchored a little way off, also heading for Van Diemen's Land, also storm-bound well after her 250 male felons had expected to depart, her officers making the same calculations of cost and strain as those of the *Sarah*. The roofs of the town were scarcely visible; decks were white with the scum of salt. For four weeks, rain tore up the sea around the *Sarah*'s hull. 'The elements formed league against us,' wrote Dr McTernan, 'at few and far between periods only, could I have the Convicts on deck, and the beds already saturated in the lower tiers were only ordered on deck to incur the hazard, I might say the certainty, of receiving additional (but a fresh supply) of wet.' It was Grummet Island afloat. The officers would not have to bring out the guns and the lash to quell mutiny here: those prisoners unused to the sea had been suffering sufficiently from nausea to render them harmless and not even James Porter, who had bolted in far less promising circumstances than these, attempted to escape the *Sarah*.

Although the delay was causing distress and extra expense, Captain Whiteside would not risk putting out. Two other transport ships bound for Australia had recently struggled out of the harbour and returned in distress shortly afterwards. Both, on their return, were investigated and condemned as unseaworthy. The *Sarah* had completed one voyage to Australia and back and was relatively young and watertight. Nevertheless, the captain knew that any ship setting out for this longest of voyages must encounter extreme temperatures, calms and storms, all with their own attendant strains on the fabric of the ship. He would be unwise to add to these unavoidable stresses the avoidable one of a severe storm in the Channel.

The voyage had not yet begun, all this lay before them and already the occupants' health aboard was suffering. Dr McTernan was a devotee of physical fitness. His regime, honed by duty on four previous voyages, was based on early rising and rugged exercise but these were not possible with water running off the decks. McTernan knew the dangers of prolonged confinement in damp berths. Although the prison-ships of the 1830s did not see the sickness and death-count of earlier vessels, sickness still lurked aboard them. Scurvy, cholera and typhus might now be rare, but the walls still oozed water, the biscuit still oozed weevil and the meat still arrived at the mess table tight with salt. Dysentery and diarrhoea killed on all ships: men o'war, merchantmen or transports, its spread blamed on 'miasma', the polluted air of cramped quarters. Constipation, too, set in quickly and was a constant, painful presence, for when the weevil did not loosen the gut, the salt took its grip on the bowels. Sometimes there was worse.

On 16 December, when the *Sarah* should have been approaching the north coast of Spain but was still waiting out the gales in the Solent, Dr McTernan was called to the orlop hold to examine Andrew Sampson, Convict No. 51, one of the men released from slavery to be sent into penal serfdom. McTernan recorded:

> A West Indian rum-drinker had a night of restlessness and rigors with flushes and thirst. He came this morning complaining of his right leg being painful. Examining I found an erythematous blush extending from the instep to the calf of the leg—very considerable tremor [?] and pain on pressure, pulse small and frequent, tongue loaded and white in the centre . . . set in motion the local abstraction of blood by the cupping glasses and copious fomentations.

Nature had turned out to aid the cause of discipline. Down on the orlop hold, where the convicts slept tightly packed in wet bunks, a flesh-eating streptococcal bacterium had been at work, burrowing into the skin of men made vulnerable by sores and lesions, scabs and tattoos; nibbling the top layer away to reveal raw, red patches. It spread, ugly and itching, sending temperatures to fever height and forcing sweat from the pores. 'Its effects,' the doctor would write at the end of a difficult voyage, 'were awe-inspiring—even on the boldest Mutineers.'

On 20 December 1836, while Dr McTernan was struggling with the first erythematics aboard the *Sarah*, the *George* left the harbour under topsails. Two days later, a month after Dr McTernan had hoped to depart, the *Sarah,* too, finally left 'under a change of wind of doubtful stability'. The wind had dropped slightly, but only slightly. It had veered to the north-north-east, a Scandinavian cold replacing the American. Out in the Channel, they 'encountered a heavy tumbling sea (the effect of the long continued westerly winds)' and a gale 'in which the Ship laboured so heavily as to take heavy Seas over the forecastle and through the hawser-holes'. With waves breaking over the top deck, the water 'flowed ... in torrents over the combings of the hatchways', snaked through the companionways, poured down the ladders and sluiced through the grated hatches to the orlop hold at the bottom of the ship, where miserable men were washed from their bunks. For a week, the weather did not change. The ship and all aboard her were sodden.

The streptococcus had continued to flourish and Andrew Sampson was still in the sick berth. He was pronounced cured just after a cold and miserable Christmas, but there was a queue for his empty sickbed. In the hospital, set up on the 'tween deck above convict quarters, Dr McTernan was working 'eighteen of my Twenty four hours', among the swelling numbers on the sick list, 'superintending cleanliness, visitation, education and cheering the desponding'. The wet, the cold and 'the usual predisposing mental condition of creatures about to be expatriated' were wreaking their effects among the convicts. Dr McTernan knew the men must get fresh air and exercise, in spite of the high winds and lashing rain, so up they went in groups throughout the daylight hours, to grope their way along the ropes and stare at the thunderous yellow sky above and the wild waters below. On 25 January, the French Canadian convict Jean Baptiste, court martialled at Three Rivers, went on deck for exercise and was knocked down by a cask that worked loose from its ropes and thundered across the deck. A half-ton of sodden oak smashed his right leg and pinned him to the rail until he was freed and carried screaming below. Tetanus infection set in and his body went into spasm. He died during the night of 27 January and his corpse went over the side in a brief ceremony the next day. A few men prayed on deck and opened their eyes to watch the coffin sink, others strained, two decks below, to hear the prayers above the groaning of the ship and their berth-mates.

Some of the convicts who had not presented with 'the blush' volunteered as Dr McTernan's 'Hospital men'. Among them was James Porter, doing his bit with the 'hailing—swabbing—scraping—stoves—hot vinegar—chloride of lime' which were Dr McTernan's weapons against the scourge. Early each morning, the doctor descended to the orlop to carry out his inspection, braced against the shuddering of the hull, squeezing among the sleeping, sick bodies with a pad steeped in herbs and vinegar held to his face against the exhalations believed to carry the disease. Each time, he found that some new instance of the creeping erysipelas blush had presented itself on one man or another and the 'Hospital men' hoisted their mates through the orlop hatch and into the sick bay.

During this harsh first month of the voyage, Porter brought himself assiduously to the attention of the officers through his work among the sick. 'I exerted myself in assisting them all I could,' he wrote, 'and keep the Prison clean from filth.' It was foul work: there were bandages and bed linen stiff with blood and pus to be doused in vinegar and washed, floorboards to be taken on deck and scrubbed, wooden walls to be scraped and disinfected. There could, however, be rewards. Having 'got great praise, from the Doctor and officers on board', Porter wrote, his irons were struck and he was allowed to go about his work with 'a loose leg', a real as well as a symbolic privilege when one of his tasks was to carry canvas slop-buckets up two flights of stairs, along the companionway and across a bucking deck to empty them over the side, returning to mop up what had gone over the edge when the ship had thrown him off balance

The erysipelas tally at the end of the voyage would be 68 cases—about one-quarter of the convicts—but the worst affected, those who succumbed most easily and stayed ill for longest, seemed to be the former West Indian slaves. The doctor, debating with himself in his log as to whether the disease could be contagious, concluded that it was not (he would later be proved wrong by researchers with greater resources) but that 'the debilitated and intemperate are more frequently its victims' and among the debilitated and intemperate were these Caribbean men of such gross and extraordinary misfortune.

Dr McTernan was at first perplexed by their presentation. The colour of their skin made it difficult for him to detect the discolouration that is the disease's first and most obvious symptom and their Creole tongue was 'as totally unintelligible as the dialect of some parts of Lancashire'. They came to him with what he thought they described as 'agues' and 'fevers' but the progress of their sickness left him in no doubt that they, too, were suffering erysipelas. First the 'West India slave Saunders-Reilly' presented himself, then 'an exceedingly delicate slave boy' known to the doctor as 'Wellington', who died from the illness. 'The former West Indian slave I St Clair, of previously intemperate habits' and the boy known only as 'Billy' all lay and suffered on their hammocks on the 'tween deck. There were also white men there, taking their sulphur quinine, their heads shaved and wrapped in fabric impregnated with camphor, shivering and crying out, for, as Dr McTernan wrote, the cause 'was planted among us by the exhalation consequent on long continued wet, between crowded decks' and black and white shared these conditions. Among those he treated were convict Pat Donelly, 'an old soldier of bad habits', court martialled in Jamaica, who was cured; Isaac Johnson, 'an old sailor and hard drinker', who died; Patrick Monahan, 'a soldier from his childhood' and 'incorrigible rum drinker, his back hardened by the lash and his heart by evil habits, a bottle of rum his smallest daily allowance', court martialled for deserting his regiment in Barbados; many others sweating and aching among them.

As the *Sarah* sailed south and the air grew dryer, suffering diminished a little on the orlop deck. For a part of each day, the hatches could now be left open for more fresh, dry air to reach the convicts there and on the 'tween deck. Linen was brought up to air in the rigging, the walls began to dry out and more time could be spent on the top deck, breathing fresh air and allowing the sun to heal the skin. They began to leave behind them the dispiriting, all-pervading smell of damp. The level of stinking, stagnant water in the bilges dropped as the amount daily expelled by the pumps was no longer equalled by the amount forced daily in by the sea. The erysipelas began its retreat from all but the most vulnerable, the sick list grew shorter and James Porter was released from the work of the 'tween-deck wards and sent instead to work aloft. This promotion to work among the sails was not a reward for his work on the wards: he had done the same thirteen years ago on the *Asia*, for no government ship was so well-manned that an extra pair of experienced hands was not welcome. Prolonged sickness such as that aboard the *Sarah* meant even half-handy convicts were welcome on the yards: one man sick put great pressure on the rest of his watch.

The second month of the *Sarah*'s voyage was an interlude of pleasant weather and all aboard made the most of it, marines, sailors and convicts storing up health against the sweats and calms of the approaching equator, and the long ocean passage which lay ahead of that. The next upset to disturb the company of the *Sarah* was caused not by nature but by man, or a combination of men. It was while James Porter was working in the sails that mysterious events occurred.

There had been strong and growing dislike for some time between James Porter and Billy Shires on the one hand, and William Cheshire and Charles Lyon on the other. Perhaps it was retrospective, but Porter would later find fault with Lyon and Cheshire as far back as their days together at Macquarie Harbour, losing no occasion in his memoirs to remark on their lack of courage, their duplicity and their untrustworthiness. He does not explain exactly where and how this dislike was born. Cheshire was a pitiable youth, easily led, selfish and perhaps despicable. Charles Lyon was uncouth and fond of his liquor but this hardly distinguished him in the milieux in which he moved: neither convicts nor Scottish seamen were noted for their sweetness. Porter himself was doubtless an irritating little so-and-so, with his boasting and swaggering and always knowing best. However, the antagonism containable when they worked together on the Sarah Island slips three years ago had hardened to vicious enmity. In Valdivia and aboard the *Blonde*, it was Charles Lyon's spite—or so Porter believed—that had scuppered his escape. He was equally unshakeable in his belief that Lyon, once more, was behind the plot aboard the *Sarah* which 'blasted all my hopes and made me a wretched object'.

James Porter would never admit that he had plotted to seize the *Sarah*. It was, he would insist even to those with an unswerving belief in his guilt, nothing but 'a wretched Conspiracy got up by two foul fiends'. As far as he was concerned, no such plan had ever existed outside the evil minds of Charles Lyon and William Cheshire. The first he knew of any such plot—he claimed—was when he was roughly roused very early one morning, marched to the quarter deck and, in the presence of Captain Whiteside and Dr McTernan, made to lie on his back with his legs upon an anvil to have his irons welded back on. They would not tell him why, but at eight o'clock, the ship was turned into the wind and came to a halt and 'all hands was called upon Deck'. When all were present, Captain Whiteside stepped forward and called out about 60 names from the informers' list. 'English, Irish, Canadians, Spanish and Italians and also a poor French Sailor that was on board did not escape the Villians . . .'

In naval tradition, the punishment was the lash. The log-line was fetched and the flogging began, starting with four dozen for Billy Shires, his back flayed to ribbons by the log-line knots. When Shires was untied to retch and gag on the deck, James Porter was called. Determined to get his say in before they tied him up and flogged him unconscious, 'I informed him, the Doctor, that I was a free man and that he would find it out as soon as we arrived at V. Diemen's Land though I was then a prisoner under his Charge and in Chains I informed him he could punish me if he thought proper, without rhyme or reason and he must put up with the consequence when we arrived at our place of destination . . .' Then he was seized and silenced by seamen and soldiers, 'lashed to a gratin and to that degree until blood hoosed from the parts where the lashings went round different parts of my person, and a lump of a black fellow flogged me across the lines and every other part of my Body until my head sank on my breast . . . nature gave way through exhaustion and [I] knew no more about it until I was cast adrift . . .' The flogging did not cease 'until 7 Bells, half past eleven o'clock being upwards of 3 hours inflicting of Torture'. The sails flapped and sighed; the boards ran red. For James McTernan, it was this prompt action and the 'timely infliction of punishment in the active members of the plot' which saved the day.

It would transpire that informers had gone to the officers the night before with news of a 'conspiracy' to seize the ship. This was the greatest obstacle to mutiny by organised gangs of convicts: not incompetence, or lack of arms or of leadership, but treachery, for there was endemic distrust among felons, carefully nurtured by their keepers. An insidious system of reward for information did more for prison discipline than the fear of punishment. It encouraged people to act on spite, to betray, to twist rumour into fact—and thus had inherent difficulties for inexperienced guards who could not tell truth from slander. The doctor was an old hand, but given the mix of old soldiers, former slaves and ship thieves on the orlop deck of the *Sarah*, his ear had been swiftly pricked when informers drifted into his dispensary to whisper their tales. James Porter had no doubt that they were Lyon and Cheshire, claiming a sailor told him that these two had gone to the captain and surgeon-superintendent to tell them that twelve Canadian convicts were plotting to rush the quarterdeck with Porter and Shires at their head to seize control of the ship 'and all were to be put to death with the exception of those who fought for their Liberty'.

However much Porter would protest Lyon's guilt and his own innocence, Dr McTernan did not believe him. Far from echoing the praise for Porter's work which Porter himself recalled, the doctor reported that his 'conduct during the voyage'—and that of the other three *Frederick* pirates—'justified the necessity of great caution'. He was convinced that mutiny had been planned and that all four of the *Fredericks* had been involved, at least before two of them turned informer. They had done it once, his thinking went, and it was natural that they would '[concert] a similar design' aboard the *Sarah* and '[succeed] in bringing many to their views', given the background of so many aboard. Worse, Dr McTernan believed that convicts had been about to make common cause with the seamen. 'In the course of enquiry into the merits of the matter,' he wrote in a report for the governor in Hobart, 'I found Wilson, one of the sailors, so unequivocally involved, not only as an abettor, but as one on whom by his solemn promise, their chief reliance rested as well for information as for aid, by conveying Arms to the Mutineers.' Perhaps James Porter and Billy Shires had not been involved in planning an uprising, but there was no doubt in the officers' minds that someone had.

Their backs shredded, Shires and Porter were carried below and put into a berth, fitted out to Dr McTernan's orders and built so small 'that it would scarcely contain us'. In this small and sweltering space, 'our feet chained together, our hands behind us, our bodies lacerated in a shocking manner', they lay and bled.

Neither Lyon nor Cheshire left any memoir of their adventures to compare with James Porter's. It is possible that the whole story of the 'wretched conspiracy' was a product of Porter's imagination or dislike. However, Lyon and Cheshire would not be the first to create a plot where none existed in order to gain the reward of denouncing it. The ship's officers appointed these two guard over Porter and Shires, during the weeks they spent chained together in the punishment berth, and Porter remembered bitterly the pleasure they took in the petty authority of the post, ensuring 'that we got neither water food nor tobbacco [sic] given to us by any of our fellow prisoners'. Ten years later, his hatred was still live when he recalled that 'that was the time [that] I craved for Death, to alleviate my tortured feelings and when describing this part of my narrative my feelings are harrowed up to such a pitch, that revenge is uppermost in my thoughts . . .'

The position of the two appointed sentinel over the men in chains was curious. Thrown into partnership by circumstance rather than choice, they had joined uneasy forces but both knew the other was capable of deceit and betrayal. So far, they had watched each other's back as well as their own, trusting no one else. Now that the plot against their two former comrades had been successfully executed, however, neither knew whether the other was still plotting. Among Alexander Pierce's gang of Macquarie Harbour runaways, each man still alive had waited for the axe to fall, wielded by the hand of a former mate. A different threat hung over the members of the little gang of two aboard the *Sarah*: the summons to the quarterdeck, the imposition of irons, the blow to hopes of an informer's pardon—for was not turning in three wanted men a greater gift to the authorities than turning in two? Lyon and Cheshire both thought they were going back to choke to death in a noose and few considerations are greater than self-preservation.

The four former shipmates spent three weeks thus, two tied together back to back, two watching over them but with a furtive eye on each other as well. The 'heat of the place added to our misery', Porter recalled, for the *Sarah* was rolling on towards the equator and each day the sun was higher in the sky, beating harder on the deck and sucking the air from the berth in which they lay. When Dr McTernan finally came and ordered the men released, 'we [had] the appearance more of anatomy's than living beings'.

On deck in the sun after their confinement, they tenderly washed each other's backs with warm water given them by sympathetic seamen. The gouges left by the log-line were beginning to heal over. For a couple of days, there was an uneasy lull aboard: others avoided them, knowing that they were trouble. Fraternisation, real or alleged, would be dangerous. The officers studied them from afar and conferred, and Dr McTernan finally sent for the men separately to ask them if they were guilty of the conspiracy for which they had been so severely punished. 'I answered him,' recalled Porter 'as he considered himself a Judge he ought to have proved it before he tortured me in the manner he had.' The rebuke seems a just one. Taking the Bible, Porter then swore that neither he nor Billy Shires had ever plotted a mutiny but that 'the Doctor would find out, the two miscreants had used this plan, with a view to make it appear to the passengers, that they have saved their lives, and the lives of all hands on board, so that by this stratagem, their lives will be spared when they reach their place of destination'.

The *Sarah* sailed on, her officers still unclear what had been planned on the orlop and in the fo'c'sle, and whether they had punished the right men. She would not stop at Rio, unlike earlier convict ships, for it was too tempting for officers to lay up and lay in stores for private trade. Too many captains and officers had neglected their ships for these temptations; there had been too many attempted mutinies in the Brazilian port. Ships were now ordered to sail direct; if they must call anywhere, the Admiralty said, it must be at Cape Town.

They headed south-east towards the African cape and the sun was hot on the boards. One afternoon, James Porter said, as he sat on deck and felt the heat on his back, the desire came to him to write a letter to 'friends' about the sad affair, his pain and suffering, the injustice of the ship's officers and the perfidy of his former mates. 'While meditating upon my truly unfortunate situation,' he began to write, laboriously scribbling, hunched over a scrap of paper filched from somewhere, 'these few lines came into my head':

> How wretched is an Exile's state of mind
> When not one gleam of hope on earth remain
> Through grief worn down, with servile chains confined
> And not one friend to sooth his heartfelt pain.
> Too true I know that man was made to mourn
> A heavy portion's fallen to my lot

With anguish full my aching heart is torn
Far from my friends by all the world forgot.
The feathered race with splendid plumage gay
Extend their throats with a discordant sound
With Liberty they spring from spray to spray
While I a wretched Exile gaze around
Farewell my Sister, Aged Aunts dear
Ere long my glass of life will cease to run
In silence drop a sympathetic tear
For your Unhappy Exiled long lost-son.
O cease my troubled aching heart to beat
Since happiness so far from thee has fled
Haste, haste unto your silent cold retreat
In clay cold earth to mingle with the Dead.

Or thus he recalled and amended them some years later—and then, from behind, came a blow and two marines fell on him, tore the paper from his hand and passed it triumphantly to their officer.

This time it was William Cheshire, striking out alone in his terrible desire for his pardon, who had gone to Dr McTernan and told him that Porter was 'writing on small pieces of Paper, and sending them round to different individuals to persuade the prisoners to rush and take the ship'. When the officer read the sad doggerel on the slip of paper he had snatched, he waved his men back, 'looked steadfastly at me and asked if the lines were my Composition, I answered yes . . . he exclaimed I feel sorrow for you, I pitty [sic] you'. Cheshire's credibility was ebbing, among officers and fellow-convicts both. When, a half-hour later, the summons came for James Porter to present himself again in the 'tween-deck dispensary for interrogation by Dr McTernan, Captain Whiteside and the senior officer of marines, Cheshire's story of passing small papers about was not mentioned. The officers went straight to the point and 'several questions were put to me concerning the capture of the Brig Frederick'.

Despite the weight of evidence proving that Porter/Conner, Shires, Lyon and Cheshire were indeed the remaining four of the *Frederick* gang, including Lord Glenelg's official notification identifying them as such, Porter still obstinately 'denied having any knowledge of it, for certain reasons of my own'. To Captain Whiteside and Dr McTernan, he insisted, as he had before his flogging, that he was a free man, wrongly accused, and would be liberated on his arrival in Hobart Town. When 'they asked me'— again and again—'if Lyons and Cheshire were ever my companions, my answer was no. The Captain said it was very strange, they should own me, and I would not own them. I made answer when we arrive at our place of destination then you will find whether I am wright [sic] or wrong'.

Porter knew, of course, that this would not happen: apart from the mass of evidence against him, there were too many people in Van Diemen's Land who could identify him as Police Number 324 as soon as he walked off the ship. 'It may appear strange,' he tells his readers earnestly, 'that I persisted in this falsehood, therefore I will give you one reason.' It was this: that even now, when others might lapse into exhaustion or apathy, James Porter was hatching one more escape plot. 'I suspected,' he explained, that 'had I informed them I was the man they represented me, they would have looked sharper after me and prevented my making an escape, for it was my intention as soon as we made the Head Land of Hobart Town to endeavour to make my escape, as I knew every Creek and Corner of it.' The plan was hopeless: the officers of the *Sarah* might have begun to suspect that Porter was innocent of the conspiracy charges but this would not persuade them that he was innocent of all others.

They rolled on towards the Australian continent on long, foaming seas and sniffed land towards the end of March: weed, birds and cloud. Three hundred miles from Sydney, the course for ships making for Van Diemen's Land departed from that of ships heading for New South Wales. Ships for Hobart Town steered a few degrees south here to find a course that would take them to within sight of Port Davey; those bound for Sydney Cove continued into the Bass Straits.

When it was judged that the *Sarah* was a week's sailing from her destination, it was William Cheshire who was called to the quarterdeck for, desperate as Van Diemen's Land approached the horizon, he had overplayed his hand badly. Two other convicts had told the officers that Cheshire had tried to persuade them to 'swear with him, that another Conspiracy was in contemplation, and if they would be staunch, he would answer that both of them would get a ticket of leave on arrival at Hobart Town'. He had gone much too far, 'this last act of his,' wrote Porter, 'had entirely overthrown all the good he considered he had done for himself'. As Hobart Town approached, all four of the *Frederick* men were made 'close prisoners' by Dr McTernan, unsure which, if any, were to be trusted.

Ninety-three days out from Portsmouth, the man at the masthead of the *Sarah* saw the south-west corner of the island through low cloud and spray. Ahead, waves that had last broken against Cape Horn were breaking against the first cliffs of Van Diemen's Land.

None aboard the *Sarah*, neither officer, seaman nor convict, knew that just ahead in the D'Entrecasteaux Channel, pieces of the *George* still swirled about the base of rocks and the bodies of 150 dead men lay in the mud below. The *George* had left Portsmouth two days before them and her voyage had been a cruel one, with convict regime and nutrition of the old-fashioned kind: ten were dead of the scurvy before they sighted Van Diemen's Land and another 50 lay scorbutic in the sick berths. Her surgeon-superintendent had belatedly told the captain that speed was paramount if they were to save 50 lives, 50 half-guineas and their reputation. Looking to save time, they had decided not to stand out around Bruny Island, but to approach Hobart Town through the narrow D'Entrecasteaux Channel between Bruny and the mainland. It would save hours crucial for the health of sick men but it was a risk, for the channel was beset by violent, unexpected gusts off the mainland hills. About 35 miles from Hobart Town, with 121 days of sailing behind them and only one or two more to go, the ship's bottom struck rocks in D'Entrecasteaux and water rushed in from below. At the enquiry, it was claimed that sentries fired down on the desperate men up to their knees in water; whether this was so or not, of the 150 who drowned, 108 were convicts.

With angry men in solitary confinement; an unfortunate, innocent French sailor in irons on suspicion of mutiny; the officers confused and half a dozen red-raw and sick on the 'tween-deck—the *Sarah* made the Heads of Hobart Town on 28 March 1837 and anchored in The Cove after a voyage of 97 days. It was an unhappy ship but at least they reached their destination.

11

The Piracy Trial

In January 1837, another British ship had dropped anchor in The Cove and offloaded distinguished passengers.

After a twelve-year reign, Lieutenant-Governor George Arthur had been removed from his post, not without putting up a fight, and had sailed for England, cheered by a vast assembly of colonists gathered at the docks to send him on his way with insults. Arthur wrote bitterly to the Colonial Office, claiming he had been calumnified: that self-interested Vandemonians had been dripping poison in ears at home and that acquaintances from his former posting in Honduras had been spreading lurid tales of 'unusual punishment' ordered under his regime there. Not so, replied Lord Glenelg soothingly, it was but the 'extraordinary duration' of his service in Van Diemen's Land which had persuaded those at home to retire him.

Glenelg was not telling the whole truth. During the three years that had passed since the ship thieves escaped Macquarie Harbour, Vandemonian life, always thick with resentment and quarrel, had become truly poisonous. Feuds were bitterly fought between the governor and those many settlers who opposed his view that the colony was first and foremost a gaol, and that all inhabitants' rights and privileges must take second place to penal security and discipline. They still wanted his chain gangs to build free roads and his muster masters to send cut-price labour to their farms and estates—but, increasingly, they wanted all this without his network of constables to patrol those roads and the interference of his magistrates in their treatment of those labourers.

As the colony developed, Arthur's refusal to allow representation of settlers' interests in his administration had been increasingly contested. Complaints about his men and methods collected on Colonial Office desks in London, for his enemies knew that undermining his reputation was one way to undermine his system. Arthur's claimed impartiality was derided: it was well known that distribution of land and convict servants depended on keeping in with the 'Arthur Faction', and that a blacklist was kept of all those who challenged his authority or disagreed, however minutely, with his policies. He was accused of an intolerance of dissent approaching tyranny. Of course, said Arthur, what gaol could permit debate? Furious letters home wrote of heavy press censorship. What gaol, replied Arthur, allows a free press? His administration was saturated in nepotism, with two of the island's most powerful men married to his nieces: Colonial Secretary John Montagu and the hated Chief Police Magistrate Matthew Forster, blind in one eye, malevolent and greedy. Naturally: information, reward and clientism were the building blocks of the totalitarian mini-state that Sir George thought needed no defending. An unsustainable difference had emerged between his view of colonial government and that of a settler population increasing in size and confidence. Administration of the colony was stymied. Sir George's time was gone. He must be recycled to governorship of Upper Canada and replaced with a mellower man.

In the place of George and Eliza Arthur and their troupe of fat sons, the *Fairlie* had brought the polar explorer Sir John Franklin. Sir John was the epitome of the bluff naval officer. He was not capacious of intellect, but brave and inspirational of loyalty in the ranks: sent to sea as a lad, gallant service seen against the French, two Arctic expeditions in search of the north-west passage behind him in which every possible hardship had been suffered—frostbite, fights with Indians, hunger, ice-jams. He was known to be fair and, unlike the martinets who governed many men o'war, to hate floggings so much that to see them caused 'trembling from head to foot' in his sturdy body.

During a recent reshuffle of colonial posts, Sir John had turned down the governorship of just-emancipated Antigua, which appointment he had been privately advised was unhealthy, ill-remunerated and subject to tedious levels of supervision by the Colonial Office. He had wished to undertake a third journey in search of the north-west passage, but, receiving no offers to finance this, agreed instead, to everyone's relief, to replace Sir George Arthur in Van Diemen's Land. Leaving Portsmouth four months before the *Sarah*, Franklin had sailed with his second wife, Lady Jane, a lively woman given to occasional light hysteria; his twelve-year-old daughter and her governess; Lady Jane's French maid; two marriageable nieces; an aide de camp; an archdeacon; and the person and family of Captain Alexander Maconochie, appointed his Private Secretary in the colony. After an uncomfortable voyage, during which Captain Maconochie perplexed his fellow passengers with the theory that Europeans used to be black and turned white as their brains developed, the party had arrived in Hobart Town to an unexpectedly tumultuous welcome. On the basis of nothing but hope and rumour, Sir John was popularly expected to turn the island into a democracy for all—apart from females, obviously; and convicts, whose labour the colonists would keep, gratis, and with disciplinary rights unchanged by any new, representative regime. Sir John and his lady spent their first weeks on the island in a whirl of banquets and balls, taken aback to be feted as liberators from Hobart to Launceston.

It was during these premature celebrations of 'liberty' that the prison-ship *Sarah* also arrived in the river with her cargo of sick and rebellious men. Dispatches, and Dr McTernan's report, were taken to Government House, the most gravely ill of the convicts were carried ashore to the Colonial Hospital and all remaining men were brought on deck, many still in chains. At midday, Police Magistrate Forster came up the ladder and walked the length of the convict ranks. Had the prisoners been well treated on the voyage? Had they any complaints? It was all as it had been thirteen years before, when Porter and Lyon came in on the *Asia* and Porter claimed to be a beer machine maker for the entertainment of his shipmates. Then, however, he had been one amongst many anonymous, dirty men; this time, his name and description were in one of the despatches just taken ashore. Two half-blind men squinted at each other and Captain Forster noted brown hair, a dimpled chin and scarred face, boxers tattooed on a left arm. Soldiers stepped forward and the captain continued down the line. If James Porter had really hoped to shimmy over the side and make for one of the headlands, there to begin his odyssey anew, his chance had gone. By half-past twelve, Police Numbers 324, 280, 819 and 299 were all on their way to Hobart gaol.

Hobart Town was bigger and busier than when the men had last seen it, almost a decade ago. The dusky bush was receding towards Mount Wellington and there were fewer reeds on the river banks than there were quays and godowns. No blacks wandered in now, for those that weren't dead were confined on Flinders Island. Nor were the kangaroo-men any longer allowed to sit on the pavements, spitting and scratching while their dogs nosed in the gutters. However, the old police gaol still stood where it had been when Charles Lyon spent a few days there after his night in the bush with Ann Ryan, and where Billy Shires and James Porter had separately waited for the Supreme Court hearings that sent them to Macquarie Harbour.

Hobart gaol, wrote one of that city's papers, was 'quite inadequate for its purposes'. First built when there were only 600 souls in the whole colony, the gaol had never been properly reconstructed to accommodate the criminal output of a population which now numbered 40,000, several of those thousands in Hobart Town alone. Conditions were bad enough for those brought in for a couple of nights off the streets. They were worse for men just arrived from a long and unhealthy voyage into the approach of Tasmanian winter. Like the eighteenth century English gaols on which it had been modelled, the compound was contained in a square about 40 yards long, surrounded by a high wall, on what had once been the edge of the town and was now in its centre and unpleasantly prominent. Debtors lived on one side, on the other, reserved for felons, there were five small cells for those awaiting execution, one 'apartment' for women and children and four larger rooms for the men, up to 250 of them at any one time. That night, the four just disembarked from the *Sarah* heard the curfew ring for the first time in three years. The next morning, they were woken by the remembered sound of the early-morning bell in the barrack yard, summoning the government-men to work. Thus would their days be regulated for a month, while the colonial justices prepared the case against them, and they were absorbed once more into convict routine.

The next Criminal Sessions was due to begin on 25 April, presided over by Chief Justice John Pedder, a Londoner who had become rich under Arthur's patronage, with an Arthur-sponsored knighthood granted and on its way to the colony. The prosecution of the ship thieves, '*Rex versus Shiers and Others*', would be undertaken by the representative of the Crown, the Solicitor General, who must now track down witnesses to the seizure of the *Frederick* and bring them to court. Captain Taw had left the colony. It was thought he had returned to Scotland. Mr Hoy, however, had transferred to Port Arthur as planned when he had recovered from his time in the bush and a request for his presence was sent down to the peninsula. William Nicholls and Mr Tate were also located and summoned.

On 26 April at nine in the morning, doors to the Hobart courtroom opened and the waiting public filed in from the cold. During the month the men had been in gaol, reports of their adventures and forthcoming trial had 'excited considerable interest', wrote one journalist sent along to cover the case, and 'the Court was excessively crowded'. They filled the time with chat until silence was called for the entrance of Chief Justice Pedder. The four *Frederick* men were not the first to appear at the bar that morning, for twelve of the previous day's prisoners had not yet received sentence. They were now brought in. Samuel French, sheep stealing: transportation for life. John Rose and William Smith, stealing from the person (picking pockets): transportation for life. William Parker, uttering a forged warrant: transportation for life. All four would be on the road gang or on their way to Port Arthur within the week. Then came Sarah Smith, another thief, similarly sentenced, 'exceedingly clamorous', who interrupted Pedder to state 'she had been most unjustly dealt with' and was told for her pains that that gentleman 'would recommend she should pass a considerable time in confinement', to which she exclaimed, 'Thank your Honour, and I hope you may sit there till I come back and be damned to you'.

At ten, the members of the jury, all soldiers, took their places. There was a pause; murmurings began again in the galleries and were allowed. At twenty past, the Solicitor General entered 'with an information in his hand' and was seen to approach the bench and there speak inaudibly to His Honour about it. Finally, the four prisoners, whom those on the pews and benches had been waiting to see, came, cuffed, to the bar. Everyone present sat forward to hear the indictment of the 'desperate men' who had been around the world and back and might be hanged in the street outside the next day.

It was the case of the Crown, represented in this small wooden room by the harassed man with thinning hair who had earlier approached the bench, that the four in the dock did . . .

> piratically and feloniously carry away, on the 30th of January 1834, the brig *Frederick*, Charles Taw, master, belonging to Our Sovereign Lord the King, and of the estimated value of £1200 from the high seas, to wit, Macquarie Harbour on the coast of Van Diemen's Land.

The first witness for the prosecution was called. He looked across the courtroom. 'I am a ship builder,' he said, 'I know the prisoners at the bar.' It was the first time the four men had seen Mr Hoy since they waved goodbye three years before and left him, sick, at Wellington Head.

The Solicitor General coaxed Hoy through the events of January, three years ago: the evacuation of the settlement, the work of the tiny party left there, the maiden voyage of the *Frederick* down the estuary and the adverse conditions at the bar; the day spent waiting for the wind to change and the eruption of armed men from the fo'c'sle at dusk. For two hours, Mr Hoy spoke of the fight in Captain Taw's cabin, the threats of pitch-pot and musket, the short, shocked voyage ashore and the night spent sleeping rough in the scrub; the bringing of food and clothes and his last sight of the *Frederick* as she crossed the bar and stood out in a north-west wind. James Porter was seen to be busily taking notes throughout.

Knowing the prisoners' defence would inevitably be that they had been coerced by others into joining the mutiny, the Solicitor General's aim was to elicit some statement from Mr Hoy that one or some of them had, on the contrary, taken an active role. Were the men before him those who had threatened to shoot? Which had he seen bearing arms? Which had he heard giving orders to the rest? Mr Hoy gave him little satisfaction. The best the Solicitor General could get was the statement that the shipwright had been 'alarmed during the disturbance, as he expected to be put to death every moment', but nothing concrete as to who had been principally responsible for this alarm was given. He had seen all four at the bar in possession of a gun or cutlass at some point but he named John Barker as the man who 'seemed to be superior' and James Lesley and Benjamin Russen as those who had threatened violence—although he thought William Cheshire might have suggested pouring hot pitch through the cabin hatch to force them out—and positively identified Billy Shires as one of those who had vetoed murder.

At just after midday, the court broke for lunch. His Honour and much of the public adjourned to various inns to discuss what they had heard, the defendants went to their cell. When Pedder had re-entered the courtroom and the audience had rustled and settled, all four had questions for the witness.

Billy Shires was given first stab at cross-examination and wished Mr Hoy to elaborate on his solicitude in ensuring adequate supplies were left. Mr Hoy confirmed Shires had personally given him a compass, a bottle of spirits and two shirts 'and told me to put them away out of sight, saying you was sorry you could not render me any more assistance'. Shires, seeking to impress the fairness of all the mutineers upon the court, also got from him the impressive list of supplies left ashore the next day—the 50 pounds of biscuit, the live goat, the pannikins and the axe. However, Mr Hoy was neutral in the face of an invitation to agree that the 'pistol' he had seen in Shires' hand was 'no more than a bar of iron'. 'What you presented at me I considered to be a loaded pistol. I might possibly have mistaken it for something else'. He refused to corroborate any ill-treatment from Captain Taw. Commandant Baylee had not left orders with *him* that the men were to be put on marine rations, said Mr Hoy, nor did he have any recollection of Shires' claim that Taw had 'held out a threat' to maroon all ten convicts in a lonely bay if they did not behave, and so that line of possible defence was closed. Shires' greatest success was in inducing Mr Hoy to agree that he believed Shires' intention in rushing into the captain's cabin—the weakest point in his personal case—was 'to save the life of those who were there and to prevent their being fired upon from above'.

Charles Lyon elicited little more.

Next up was James Porter, who referred to his neat and copious notes and also pressed home the generosity of the provisions left 'with a view to show, that when the brig was captured, she could have had but a very small quantity, after deducting what was sent on shore'. He also prompted Mr Hoy to remember that when the men had left him on shore for the last time, 'Mr Hoy said to him that the humanity and kindness he had received from the prisoners was so great and unexpected, that he could not forget it'. According to one newspaper report, Porter's cross-examination was 'conducted with considerable acuteness'.

The same journalist who watched and characterised Billy Shires as 'a quiet man' and Porter and Lyon 'intelligent—what may be termed "smart" men', described William Cheshire, last of the defendants to speak, as 'a weak lad'. His examination, inevitably, 'referred to his character' and Mr Hoy's promise to 'procure him some indulgence'. 'You was sent to me as a boy,' Mr Hoy confirmed, 'and was with me three years; your conduct was generally as good as most persons in your situation.' It was not much of a recommendation, although Hoy did add that Major Baylee had authorised him to promise all the men that 'if you behaved well, that when you came to Hobart Town, something would be done for [you]'.

James Tate, the free man who had acted as first mate, now took the stand, corroborated Mr Hoy's description of events and swiftly incriminated Lyon, Shires and Cheshire: the first had suggested they 'lift up the hatch and fire down the skylight'; the second 'presented a pistol to me [and] said not a word I'll blow your brains out'; the third he saw 'standing with a musket'. He had not seen James Porter armed but it had been Porter who had tied his hands behind him, thus taking an active part in events. Shires would not cross-examine, saying Tate 'would swear anything'. Lyon got from him a general corroboration of Captain Taw's uncouth and incompetent behaviour, particularly his drunkenness, but could not get him to confirm the captain had actually kept back rations, nor that he had behaved in so vicious a manner as to excuse disobedience from the men.

After a brief examination of William Nicholls, Mr Hoy's convict servant, the Solicitor General rested his case and Justice Pedder questioned him about the 'information' he had passed to the bench that morning. The exchange was of little interest to the public, which had been gripped by the unfolding story of mutiny, but the answer to Pedder's questions would turn out to be more important to the men's fate than anything elicited during the day's interrogation and cross-examination of witnesses. Could 'the place where the capture took place', Pedder asked, 'properly [be] described as the high seas, or not?' The Solicitor General 'contended it was properly described' but Pedder was not convinced and 'the point was reserved'.

At nine at night, the defendants were finally asked if they had anything to say in their defence before sentence was passed. With the black cap placed ready and a death sentence minutes away, all four claimed 'that they were compelled to join the mutiny'. Shires was 'obliged to act as he had done, through fear of others who were on board'. Lyon had been 'ordered to navigate the vessel', so had William Cheshire and James Porter, who further claimed that the whole thing had been caused by 'those who had charge of the vessel and crew not following the orders left with them by Major Bailey [sic]'. All four dwelt on their gentlemanly treatment of those put ashore, spoke of the hardships they had faced on their adventures and 'avowed they had given themselves up to the Government there'. Each ended his statement 'by throwing himself upon the mercy of the Court and the Jury'.

Before the jury retired to consider its verdict, Chief Justice Pedder addressed its members on the technical points he had earlier raised with the Solicitor General. First, piracy could only take place aboard vessels on the high seas, but was the *Frederick* on the high seas when she was seized? If the answer to this question was no (an estuary not being considered 'high seas') then the men at the bar were not guilty of piracy. Furthermore, Pedder asked, could the *Frederick* justly be termed a 'brig' or any other type of vessel, or did she have to be legally registered as such before the term could apply? Was it not more proper to describe her as 'a quantity of wood and other materials so fastened as to possess the means of becoming a brig, but possessing no one constituent necessary to justify those materials being then so called'? Finally, could the prisoners justly be termed 'mariners' and could their activity be termed 'mutiny'? Their being 'mariners' depended on the existence prior to the crime of a specific relationship in law between crew and officers; their activity being 'mutiny' depended on there having been an individual legally in command of the brig (if such the *Frederick* was, and not just a bundle of floating bits). Captain Taw had been due to take command when the *Frederick* went to sea but if she had not yet gone to sea, he was not yet in command; which left Mr Hoy the shipbuilder in charge, and disobedience to a shipbuilder did not constitute mutiny.

John Pedder had offered the twelve men a way out of their impasse: few juries, even in this carelessly violent country, even composed of soldiers, liked to convict prisoners of capital crimes unless there was clear evidence of violence or determination to re-offend. The jury deliberated for an hour and as soon as they returned the judge asked:

'Have you reached your verdict?'

'We have, Your Honour.'

'How do you find the prisoners?'

'Guilty, Your Honour . . .'

' . . . but,' said the foreman, the jury was 'of the opinion, the offence was not committed on the high seas, nor were the prisoners *mariners* on board the *Frederick*, but were only men *employed as mariners* to work the vessel'. Chief Justice Pedder and his advisors would not have known it, but they had offered a similar loophole to the *Frederick* men that the Chilean Secretary for Foreign Affairs had proposed in September. Then, Colonel Walpole had resisted, now, a Vandemonian jury had accepted the interpretation.

With these reservations expressed by Pedder and seconded by the jury, the day could not end with the sentence of immediate execution that the defendants and many of those watching had expected. Nonetheless, a guilty verdict had been pronounced. Thirty-five-pound irons were fastened around the men's ankles and they were taken away, exhausted from their twelve-hour day in court. Finally, back in the gaol, answering the curiosity of the cell-mates who had seen them off that morning, debating the implication of the jury's words, eyeing Lyon and Cheshire on the other side of the crowded room, James Porter and Billy Shires 'comforted each other as well as our situation would allow'. There was little enough comfort to be had: they did not know how long they would spend there, nor whether the jury's remarks were sufficient to oblige Justice Pedder to pass a non-capital sentence, nor, indeed, what happened next beyond many more nights spent shackled and lying on cold stone and straw.

There was one hope, and they clung to it. 'Woe be to us if the bloodthirsty Arthur had ruled,' wrote Porter, recalling this moment nine years later, 'had not the Colony been under the Government of the human Sir John Franklin,' they would, he believed, have been immediately hanged. It was a judgement that neither Sir John nor Sir George fully deserved. Arthur's last despatch, written three days before his ignominious departure, had asked that the names of 337 meritorious convicts be laid before His Majesty 'for approbation of absolute or conditional pardons' and Franklin, kindly man though he was, had discovered that there were far more pressing things to concern him than the fate of four possible pirates in the lock-up. Determining the exact nature of this crime, and its due punishment, was not the sort of problem that appealed to the new man. It was decided that the whole perplexing but minor question of the four ship thieves would be sent to London for legal advice. It would mean painful delay and indefinite confinement for the defendants but would be one fewer problem to detain the new administration as it struggled through the sticky webs of intrigue which were Vandemonian politics and applied itself to defusing the hopes raised by Arthur's departure.

The two-headed fever for reform and abolition emanating from Britain in the 1830s had assumed unexpected shapes as it drifted across the world in ships, gossip, newspapers and garbled report. In Jamaica, it produced the premature uprising of slaves; in the colonies, it bolstered calls for emancipation from London and a measure of home rule with some representative body composed of local residents. London had no such plans, and would have been alarmed at their suggestion. Certain influential groups in and around Westminster were indeed beginning to plan a major change to the Australian colonies, but self-government was no part of their programme.

The anti-transportation movement in Britain had, for many years, found it frustratingly difficult to extract information from the penal colonies that was untainted by interest or spite. Wildly different versions of the convict's lot were sent back in answer to their questions, all stated as absolute truths: they were shamefully pampered; they were treated worse than slaves; their labour was productive; it held back the development of the colony; convict women were prone by character to sexual excess; they were unprotected and forced into prostitution. The appointment of Alexander Maconochie to Van Diemen's Land had offered the opportunity to commission data from a fresh and relatively neutral source. Before leaving Britain, he had been asked by the Society for the Improvement of Prison Discipline, an influential charity concerned with penal reform, to complete a 67-point questionnaire on the condition of the prisoners in Van Diemen's Land. Maconochie's political masters agreed to this request as long as his report was vetted by Sir John Franklin and the Colonial Office.

Shortly after the ship thieves' trial, he submitted the first draft of this report to Franklin. It had been heavily influenced both by his dislike of the overbearing colonists who tried to force themselves into positions of power and wealth and his conversations with the Quaker missionary, James Backhouse, who had been so appalled at conditions in Macquarie Harbour and elsewhere. As Maconochie collated his findings for the charitable Society at home, the outraged tone of their criticism seeped into his own. Maconochie could rival Sir George Arthur in his passion for paper. Sir John Franklin, concerned to be fair, invited rebuttals of Maconochie's first draft from settlers and colonial officials who disagreed with him. When these, in their turn, were handed to Maconochie, the pile of paper amassed was enormous and Maconochie decided to write a summary of his own findings, which would otherwise be lost in the reams of text. This last file Franklin failed to check—but it was this unchecked and private memo, thorough in its condemnation of 'the System', that was plucked from the bundle in February 1838 and passed to the Home Secretary and critic of transportation, Lord John Russell. He knew exactly what to do with it.

Big questions were being discussed in committee rooms in London, but the lesser ones of the high seas, the registration of a colonial brig and the position in law of the shabby men who worked her, raised in Hobart and sent to England, were no nearer resolution. While they waited for the 'English justices' to work out the answers, the four ship thieves were detained once more in Hobart Police Gaol and this was no less miserable a place to be as summer approached than when they had first been locked inside to shiver through the winter. Once a day, they and the other male felons were allowed exercise in a courtyard 'where the stench is occasionally enough to bring on disease'. Once a fortnight, they were taken to divine service. Other excitements were few: there were fights, card games, visits from lawyers and journalists, and occasional supplies of liquor and tobacco brought in from outside. Each week, the numbers swelled and diminished with the rhythm of the magistrates' sessions and news was brought back of floggings, imprisonment and fines; each month came the greater pomp of the Criminal Sittings and news of graver punishments: the noose, the road gang or Port Arthur.

Porter and his fellow ship thieves had lived in this dim squalor for six months when a ship came in from London with news that raised hopes in the gaol and gripped the community outside its walls. King William IV of Britain was dead and his niece, the High and Mighty Princess Alexandrina Victoria, had become queen. In Hobart Town, the oath of allegiance was ceremonially administered to Sir John Franklin by the senior military officer of the colony, there were gun salutes at Signal Point and *feux de joies*, parties in Government House and a procession down Elizabeth Street. In the gaol, there was feverish speculation, for everyone knew that coronations, births, weddings and other royal occasions traditionally saw the exercise of clemency, with pardons granted to well-supported or repentant criminals. Lists were indeed being drawn up in Franklin's office of convicts who had helped put down a recent outbreak of bushranging round Campbelltown, others who had helped save lives in accidents in the harbour, and others still, whose age and infirmity rendered their labour useless to the Crown. The ship thieves waited, but no news was brought to the Police Gaol that their names were among those being put forward for reprieve.

It was just after these celebrations, and the disappointment that followed them, that James Porter asked for and was given pen and paper. He had not given up hope: he had dodged his punishment before and was determined to dodge it again. If Sir John's office would not forward a request for pardon, he was going to make sure one got back to London by a different route.

The account of the seizure of the *Frederick* which he scribbled down in his communal cell was a brief and simple one, written without flourishes. It concentrated on the two days in which the *Frederick* was seized, with few details of the voyage or the life in Chile that followed, other than those of dangers passed and sufferings endured, calculated to arouse sympathy and admiration.

Whether Porter was conscious of it or not as he wrote, it is clear that his developing defence consisted not only of an account of his own bravery and courage but also of Charles Lyon's baseness. The methods that Lyon and Cheshire had used aboard the *Sarah* were turned against them in Hobart gaol. Lyon makes his first appearance (on page two) in confinement in Macquarie Harbour 'where he had been placed for using threats and behaving insolently to the captain'. Was there not mutiny in the making here? When the *Frederick* set off down the estuary on her voyage to Hobart, 'contentment appeared on the countenances of all on board, with the exception of Charles Lyon'. Surely another sign of villainy? Porter himself was still innocent of any knowledge of the plot. Put ashore to do his laundry, he 'observed many of the prisoners whispering together and laughing, but had not the slightest suspicion of their designs'. In the fo'c'sle after supper, he 'was asked to sing a song'; when the mutiny began, he was 'ordered' by Mr Fare to stand upon the forescuttle hutch and guard the soldiers taken prisoner below. Someone else had set afoot the mutiny and Porter had been haplessly caught up. His friend was not forgotten: when others had been set on violence, it had been Billy Shires, said Porter, who had insisted on treating the captain and Mr Hoy decently, prevented their being shot out of hand in the captain's cabin and ensured that the rations were fairly divided the following day. This narrative, dated 'Gaol Hobart', 1st November 1837, was sent to Sir John Franklin's office with the hope it might be forwarded to London to sway the deliberations of the 'English justices' in the men's favour.

The audience in James Porter's mind as he reinvented himself (and put in a word for his mate) was the British Home Secretary, but another man in Hobart Town saw a different market for his work.

William Gore Elliston had been in the colony for seven years. He was a man of flair and entrepreneurial spirit, who had come from managing the Royal Theatre in Drury Lane to owning a shop and liquor store, first in the bush town of Bagdad and then in more prestigious premises in Hobart. He had become an auctioneer on the back of selling the liquor business and then turned a nice profit educating the sons of gentlemen at a private academy. His most recent and ambitious business venture had been the acquisition of the *Hobart Courier*. This had cost him the considerable sum of £12,000, which he needed to start recouping. Mr Elliston had a sharp eye for an earner. Only two months after the new governor's arrival, his journal was advertising for sale a handsome work in twelve parts: *The Voyages and Travels of Sir John Franklin*, with 'a splendid portrait of His Excellency'. His man had been in court on 26 April to cover the piracy trial, now, spotting Porter's story as another potential hook for readers, Elliston decided to run it as a serial in the newly renamed *Courier*.

It was Elliston who gave Porter's blunt essay its enticing title: *A Narrative of the sufferings and adventures of certain of the convicts who piratically seized the Frederick at Macquarie Harbour in Van Diemen's Land, as related by one of the pirates, whilst under sentence of death in the gaol at Hobart Town*. It was also Elliston who, in 1838, sliced it into thirteen episodes and fed it to consumers of vice and scandal in his adopted city. Perhaps it was he who suggested the cliffhanger to James Porter, the last paragraph of whose appeal, as it appeared in the *Courier*, was calculated to keep readers interested in the outcome of his story even after serialisation had finished: 'we have every reason to believe', he wrote, that our 'sentence of death will be commuted to transportation for life and our case has gone home for opinion of the English judges'.

It was as well that William Elliston had taken a hand in the game. In December 1837, some report on the men's case had been seen in London by Colonial Secretary Lord Glenelg and forwarded to Lord

John Russell, for it was he, as Home Secretary, who put forward names recommended for pardon to the Crown. This report has disappeared from Home Office records so we do not know what summary was made of the case by Franklin's office, nor whether James Porter's manuscript was later forwarded to London to be added to it. However, Glenelg's covering letter to Russell mentions that a report by Dr McTernan was part of the bundle, and in the doctor's eyes the men were guilty of everything imputed to them, and probably more besides. No reply came from the Home Office, or none has survived. In October 1838, when the four had been in Hobart gaol for a year and a half, it was a copy of William Elliston's journal that brought the matter back to the Colonial Secretary's attention. In this newspaper 'narrative', Lord Glenelg wrote to Sir John Franklin, 'it is stated that shortly after their arrival in the Colony they were placed on their trial before the Chief Justice for the piracy, found guilty and sentenced to be hanged, which sentence they had every reason to believe would be commuted to transportation for life. I should wish,' he went on, apparently forgetting that the matter had passed across his own desk several months previously, 'to receive some report of the fate of those convicts, assuming the sentence of death to have been commuted, as was expected.' Their case had been archived for 18 months: a short time in the affairs of government; a longer one for men living on stone floors and eating skilly in Hobart gaol.

Franklin's report on their case had been pushed way down the list of Home and Colonial Office priorities by the arrival of Maconochie's far more important manuscript. In the same month in which the ship thieves had appeared in court in Hobart, the Molesworth Committee had begun its deliberations in London. With Lord John Russell's active sponsorship, the committee's agenda was clear from the start: its members wanted an end to transportation and they were looking for material that would support their case. Maconochie's memo, as Russell had immediately realised, was just the stuff. It contained indictment after indictment of what he had found in Van Diemen's Land: assignment was 'cruel, uncertain, prodigal; ineffectual either for reform or example', riddled with cronyism and a 'lottery of punishment'; discipline could only be enforced by an 'extreme severity' which was distasteful to the feelings of the age; convictry held back colonial development by free emigrants with a stake in their land and labour; the System as a whole encouraged immorality among convicts and convict masters alike; it was a stain on Britain's reputation. It must end.

If 'the English judges' ground their justice slowly, the court of British public opinion did not. When Lord John Russell had Maconochie's memo printed and made public, the press seized on it and gave the whole country the opportunity to share his disgust with what he had found in the Antipodes. From that moment on, there could be only one outcome of the enquiry into the future of transportation enquiry. From the moment news of Maconochie's 'betrayal' became known in Van Diemen's Land, there could equally be only one outcome in the staffing arrangements at Government House.

Had Maconochie not had the protection of his official position in September 1838, he would have been lynched when British newspapers airing opinions ascribed to him were brought ashore in Hobart. With no warning—for his memo had never been made public in the colony—the free and emancipated population found their society denigrated as morally degenerate and themselves accused of slave-owning tyranny. Maconochie refused to recant. Faced with furious protest from an island threatening ungovern-ability, Sir John Franklin was finally obliged to dismiss him. He, his wife and his six children could stay in their quarters for the time being, but he was removed from any participation in public affairs.

While an unwelcome spotlight was shone upon 'the System' in Van Diemen's Land in 1838, the case of the four men in Hobart gaol did not receive attention until the beginning of the next year. Presumably Lord Glenelg had jogged Lord John Russell's memory of the case when his own was nudged by Elliston's newspaper, for a cursory reply was eventually sent. The envelope conveyed to Sir John Franklin from a ship in the River Derwent in July 1839 contained two papers. The first, overturning doubts over high seas and mariners, was an order for the men's execution. The second was permission for Sir John, 'should he see fit', to remit the sentence. After two years' delay, the buck had been passed back to Hobart.

On 16 July, the *Colonial Times* reported that the final decision on the four men's future was taken. 'The doom,' it wrote, 'of the pirates, who have been so many months in gaol, is at last fixed. They are to expiate their offences, by a residence at Norfolk Island, for the term of their natural lives.' It was not a judgement of which the newspaper could approve. 'The majesty of the laws,' it observed, 'would have been fully maintained had an act been passed respecting them, upon the accession of Her Majesty Queen Victoria to the throne.' Although the editor praised Sir John Franklin for taking 'the humane course, instead of shedding their blood', he was in no doubt of the nature of the men's pardon: 'their doom is hopeless captivity in the Island of Demons, which is only to be equalled by the infernal regions of Dante'.

Now things moved swiftly. At the end of that month, James Porter, Billy Shires, Charles Lyon and William Cheshire embarked a schooner in Hobart harbour. In Port Jackson, Sydney, they transhipped to the *Governor Phillip*, bound for Norfolk Island. It was their fourth voyage in chains.

12

The Infernal Regions

If Macquarie Harbour had been a nigh perfect gaol for its 300 men, penned in by bush and sea, how much more so was Norfolk Island for its 1400 sinners: a volcanic outcrop 1000 miles from the eastern coast of New South Wales, eight miles long by five across, with nowhere to hide, no harbours and ocean on every side.

Covered in enormous pines, backlit by the evening sun 'like the bronzed spires of some vast cathedral', encircled by blue water, blue horizon and a blue sky, Norfolk Island had been a place of primeval loveliness. Its air was perfumed by jasmine, looping through the woods in muscular tangles, and, before the Europeans came, disturbed only by wind, the thrum of surf and birdsong. The first white visitors, landing 50 years before Porter arrived, had planted sweet things which throve there: sugar cane, guava, lemons and figs. Beautiful as it was, however, this little island inspired disgust and terror, for these few square miles of loveliness were home to the most degraded prisoners received or created by 'the System', '1400 doubly-convicted prisoners, the refuse of both penal colonies', whose 'condition', as Sir William Molesworth had just written in his report, was 'one of unmitigated wretchedness'.

On 26 August 1839, in cold midwinter weather, the *Governor Phillip* hove-to off Cascade, the island's principal landing place, and lines were sent ashore. Every man aboard went along them, bludgeoned by spray. On the beach, they stripped naked and lined up in the blustery winds for yet another surgeon to examine them and note their distinctive features in the latest set of records. When his remarks had been taken down by another set of convict clerks, they dressed and were marched to the commandant's office in the grim penal village of Kingston, the island's only settlement. There, as if on cue, a vignette of Norfolk Island life was played out before them. 'The moment I landed,' Porter would write, 'a man was being dragged before [the officer] with irons on he could scarce crawl in, and before he could reach the office he ordered him 50 lashes without even inquiring into the case.'

That afternoon, another commandant, Major Bunbury, delivered a brief speech to the new arrivals, marshalled into rows in the barracks' yard by soldiers poking them with muskets. His was the formal introduction to life on Norfolk Island: the latest set of warnings, rules, threats of punishment, half-hearted promises of privilege for good behaviour. The less formal induction came later, at night, when the newcomers were locked into the cells with the 'Old Hands', and found out how the island was run on the other side of the gaol wall. This, too, was all predictable to men with the ship thieves' accumulated years in the system: there were gangs and gangleaders, favourites and catamites, bullies and the bullied, the 'stone men' who would not give in even under the lash and those others who for 'a stinking piece of Tobacco', would run to the guards with 'every trifling occurrence of the day, hatch[ing] lots and form[ing] conspiracies into which the unwary were ensnared'.

The tactics and hierarchies were familiar but the conditions in which Porter and his companions found they were to live were the worst yet encountered in a lifetime of gaols and labour camps. Even Grummet Island and the Derwent River chain gangs could not compare with the brutality and the humiliations devised and inflicted by the Norfolk Island regime. 'In every way,' the next Island commandant but one was to write, disgusted by what he found there, the prisoners' 'feelings were habitually outraged, and their self-respect destroyed.' Servility was enforced, with all convicts 'required to cap each private soldier whom they met, and even each empty sentry-box which they passed'. If they met an officer, 'they were to take off their caps altogether, and stand aside, bare-headed, in a ditch if necessary, and whatever the weather, until he passed'. They were penned like animals, 'cooped up at night in barracks which could not decently accommodate half the number'; fed and watered like animals, 'neither knives, nor forks, nor hardly any other conveniences were allowed at their tables. They tore their food with fingers and teeth and drank for the most part out of water buckets', and were punished like animals, 'for the merest trifles . . . flogged, ironed or confined in gaol for successive days on bread and water'. It was clear, said Porter, that here 'Tyranny and Cruelty was in its vigour'.

James Backhouse, the Quaker missionary who had visited Macquarie Harbour years before, had also spent time on Norfolk Island and had told Alexander Maconochie and the Molesworth Committee of men perverted by despair. His stories, too, were familiar: the man who 'doubted the being of a Deity, but wished, if there was a God in heaven, that he would deprive him of life'; the convicts who killed each other 'apparently without malice, and with very slight excitement', in order to be sent to Sydney and hanged. The language of offenders when challenged revealed the same hopelessness that had permeated Macquarie Harbour: they were 'weary of life'; they 'preferred death because there was no chance of escape'; they 'knew they should be hanged, but it was better than being where they were'.

Successive rulers of Norfolk Island, left to their own devices by the mainland government, had exercised arbitrary and absolute power. An apt perversion had emerged among those governed by their caprice—suicide by lottery. A gang of convicts would draw straws. The first to draw a short straw was to die. The second was to be his killer. All the rest would be shipped as witnesses to Sydney, as there was no judge on the island competent to hear cases of murder. One of the gang would already be dead, another would hang and the rest would have a respite from the Island, and perhaps a chance of escape into the mainland bush. The game rested on the agreement of all participants to die and many gave it, for here there was no hope of reform: not the prospect of a ticket of leave which animated convicts in New South Wales; nor the reports of abolition which had roused the slaves of the West Indies; not even the dull grind and slip of Governor Arthur's system of reward and punishment.

Yet even on Norfolk Island, where nature and man were in relentless league against them, there were convicts driven by the thought of escape. Some persuaded their mates to hack off their toes with a hoe in order to get to the hospital. Others ate poisonous berries, or rubbed noxious substances into their sores to produce ulcers. A few put out their own eyes. Others not so prepared for self-inflicted agony made attempts at ship-thievery. Small boats, used by the officers to go to outlying rocks to fish, were taken. The fugitives were always pursued, and the oarsmen lashed; or they sank under gunfire or waves and all aboard men were drowned. Other men snuck by night to caves with pieces of stolen wood and attempted to build a boat. Informers brought every one before the commandant, where they were flogged. Still there were men obsessed, their 'passions', wrote James Backhouse, 'centred in one intense thirst for liberty, to be gained at whatever cost. Their faces were like those of demons'.

Five years before the *Governor Phillip* delivered the ship thieves, there had been a brief and unsuccessful mutiny on the Island: the convicts planned to rise, hang and quarter the officers, rape their wives and sail for America. The man who finally goaded them into uprising was Commandant Colonel Morisset, an unrestrained sadist, governor from 1829 to 1834. His regime had seen the worst of the depraved and sickening games that made Norfolk Island notorious, dependent on the utter futility of the victims' protest, the utter impunity of the practitioners and the encouragement of a charismatic and morally rotten leader. The mutiny plot was uncovered when Morisset was unhinged by mental illness and confined to bed and so it was his second in command who earned the name of Flogging Fyans.

After a final burst of frenzied cruelty, Morisset and Fyans were removed and replaced by Major Anderson, who was sane but clove to the lash in his sanity as Morisset had in his madness. 'The gracious God,' wrote the island's chaplain, whose protests went ignored, 'who heareth the sighing of the prisoner, and who avengeth, will, if he has not already, summon to his account, Joseph Anderson who was Commandant at Norfolk Island.' He had been replaced by Major Bunbury, the man who had ordered the 50-stroke flogging without enquiry on the day of Porter's arrival.

James Porter and the others arriving on the *Governor Phillip* had only to endure Bunbury's regime for three months, for in October he relinquished his post to Major Ryan. It was time enough for Porter to describe him as 'a second Nero' for his indifference to the brutalities carried out on his orders. Ryan's was the last short-term appointment to this unwanted post and he was the best man to take it so far. The excesses of arbitrary power ended with his arrival; 'he proved himself to be', said Porter, 'as much the father to the poor exiles as Bunbury did, the Brute', but it was always known that the appointment of this decent man was temporary. Ryan himself sought to reassure the prisoners that the old ways would not be brought back. Walking unguarded among them, as Major Baylee had done at Macquarie Harbour, he assured the men that the next governor 'would soon make his appearance among us and that he was a better and a kinder Commandant than himself', but there was little faith in such words on Norfolk Island.

This promise, however, would prove against all the odds to be different. While Porter, Shires, Lyon and Cheshire learnt the ropes of the Kingston barracks and labour gangs, their hated new home was being much discussed in Sydney and London. They did not yet know it, but they had been sent to the Island of Demons just in time to participate, briefly, in one of the oddest experiments in penal Australia, presided over by one of the oddest men to be given power there.

Transportation to parts beyond the seas had been condemned by parliamentary committee, press and public opinion as inefficient and inhumane. In Britain, it had been decided that the mechanisms for sending convicts to New South Wales would be wound down. Penitentiaries on the modern, American model would be the new system of punishment and reform. Until these were built, however, some convicts, at least, must continue to be sent overseas and somewhere must be chosen to house them. Norfolk Island was to be retained for this purpose, for 'the healthiness of the climate, the fertility of the soil, and its entire separation from intercourse with ordinary emigrants, render it', thought the Colonial Office, 'peculiarly fit for [their] reception'. However, given the shocking stories of abuse that had been recently related to the Molesworth Committee and aired in the British press, London was adamant that there must be 'an essential alteration . . . in the system of punishment pursued there'. There must be no more Morissets and Andersons. Henceforth, convicts must be governed by some officer 'who should feel a deep interest in their moral improvement' and 'be disposed to devote his whole energies to this important object'. The man confidentially recommended for this task was Alexander Maconochie who, in enforced idleness in Hobart Town, had spent his time forwarding avant-garde theories of rehabilitation and reform to Lord John Russell, with pleas to be allowed to try them out somewhere in the changing colony. It was decided that he would be given charge of Norfolk Island, under strict conditions, as a laboratory for his experiments.

On 6 March 1840, therefore, the captain, his wife and their six children stepped ashore on Norfolk Island to be welcomed by Major Ryan. With them were 250 convicts newly arrived from England, not even disembarked in Sydney. These were the men allotted to Maconochie as guinea pigs. Known as the 'New Hands', they were to be housed at the opposite end of the island from the 'Old Hands', in a purpose-built compound called Longridge. Maconochie's orders were that this was to be kept segregated from the depraved and double-convicted souls already on the island, whose influence was otherwise expected to work perniciously upon them, and that his experiments in penal management were to be confined strictly to this small group.

For the first few days of the captain's tenure nothing changed in Kingston. There were rumours that he had brought some strange new system to the other end of the island but it was known that the Old Hands were excluded from it. They continued with the drinking buckets, the open privies, crowded barracks and overseers. Very soon, however, the striding, energetic figure of the new commandant was seen and heard in Kingston, too, inspecting, conversing, questioning, informing. He was shocked by what he saw and heard there. Never one to tread carefully, within days of arrival he had decided that he could not reform this 'brutal, turbulent hell', as Major Ryan had tried to do, with more food, more time in the allotments, milder punishments and better supervision. Rather, he would sweep it away altogether.

Shortly after the New Hands had been disembarked, the ship thieves were rounded up along with the other Old Hands and brought to the Kingston barrack yard to hear their new governor speak. When Maconochie entered and saw them gathered there, even the determined captain faltered. 'Almost the most formidable sight I ever beheld,' he wrote, 'was the sea of faces up-turned to me when I first addressed them.' Their eyes were sunken and stony with hate. They were dirty, ragged and scarred; a sour smell moved around and above them.

The captain, raising his voice against the wind in the pines, started with a pleasant but bland statement.

> It has been the pleasure of our most gracious Queen to forward me to this Island for the purpose of ascertaining how far the system of discipline by which [you] have for many years been governed is susceptible of improvement. Your wretched condition and mutinous proceedings have given rise to a deal of anxiety on the opposite side of the Globe and I am truly gratified to learn from [Major Ryan] that the removal of the Evils and abuses which he had found to exist have in so short a time produced something like a reformatory change among you.

So far, so predictable. There was not a man in the crowd who had not already heard vague promises of reform and words of good intention at some stage in his penal career and who found the reality to be a return to the yoke and the lash. The regime that Maconochie had introduced at Longridge, however, and had decided to extend, would—if allowed to run its course—be truly different. As he explained it to them that day, it held out the prospect of freedom, and this was something that the Norfolk Island lifers thought they had lost forever.

Maconochie's proposal to Lord John Russell had been that transportation sentences should no longer be measured out in years, but in units of some currency which convicts might earn and pay back at a speed determined by their own labour. This currency he called 'Marks' and this was the experimental system he had been authorised to manage among the New Hands at Longridge. 'Those that earned 6000 marks', as he now explained to the men in the barrack yard, 'would discharge a seven years' sentence or 7000 would be required for ten years' servitude'; 8000 would pay off a sentence of life. A portion of their 'earnings' might be 'given up along the way in exchange for luxuries', or the whole might be set aside 'to hasten their discharge. While the escape of the incorrigible would be barred for ever', Maconochie warned, he 'would delight to hasten the freedom of the worthy'.

What the captain was proposing was a revolution in the relationship between a prisoner and his sentence. Few were on Norfolk Island for anything less than life and the only dim prospect of release hitherto had been in the exercise of 'mercy', 'clemency' or 'pardon': terms which emphasised dependence less on their own behaviour than on charity in the chain of personalities that stretched between them and the Crown. Maconochie's system seemed to offer responsibility for their own futures, untainted by others' whim or interest. When these implications were absorbed, the men's reaction was profound. The new commandant's speech, wrote Thomas Cook, a convict present that day, 'drew Tears from the Eyes of the most hardened and depraved beings. The cheers which emanated from the Prisoners were deafening.'

So overwhelmed were the Old Hands that the warning in the last part of the captain's speech went unremarked. Maconochie did tell the men before him that 'he did not then hold the authority of Her Majesty's Government to extend [the Marks system] to us as re-convicted men', rather than prisoners arriving fresh from England, but he also assured them that he had 'no hesitation in saying that he should find little difficulty in obtaining such an authority and that he would venture therefore to place us under that System with the English prisoners [at Longridge] until the pleasure of the Government was known'. Optimism had blinded the captain, or he was trying to force his seniors' hands with a fait accompli. In Kingston, it seemed as if James Porter and his companions in misfortune had been given back the chance of a decent life but the extension of the Marks system to the Old Hands working out sentences fixed under the old terms was impracticable and completely unauthorised: neither Sydney nor London had any idea of what Maconochie was doing.

There was little immediate change after the great speech, but much hope. The unseen New Hands remained in Longridge and the Old Hands remained in Kingston, going about their usual tasks. More men were allowed allotments to grow their own vegetables, and more time off government work to cultivate them; some steps towards improving hygiene were undertaken and eating utensils were issued but it was not until the last week of May that they realised how radical their commandant intended the changes in Norfolk Island life to be.

On 25 May, they woke to find all the prison gates standing open and the overseers telling them there was to be no work that day, but only celebration and joy. It was the birthday of the young queen, and Maconochie had decided this would be a public holiday for all, felon and free. Some could not comprehend it, and lingered fearfully inside the prison yards, uncertain what to do with a day not ordered by the whip and the plough; but as their fellows walked out and did not return, and there were sounds of talk and laughter, even the most craven and brutalised followed. They went down to the beach, and stared at the surf, noticing the brilliance of sun and water on which free visitors to the island had often remarked. They wandered round the fields. At midday, special food was brought out and they were encouraged to build fires and grill their fresh pork. Captain Maconochie walked genially among them, chatting and encouraging and speaking of the queen's concern for their welfare. At long trench tables, vats of rum and lemon appeared to toast her, paid for by Maconochie. Then the fires were doused, the tables cleared away and handbills passed among scarred and clumsy hands, with thumbs disfigured by torture. There was to be an entertainment. The old lags sat in wondering rows, turning the papers over and over, looking furtively at Captain Maconochie and his family, dressed in their best, and equally furtively at the overseers who under a different rule had tied them up, flogged them, raped them, thrown salt water on their scars and set food and water too far away for a trussed and crawling man to reach. They had not forgotten that under Major Anderson, the offence of 'Singing a Song' could be punished with 100 lashes.

James Lawrence, London fraudster, stood up to sing a selection of songs from 'the admired Comic Opera of the Castle of Andalusia', with a backing group of ten. Others sang 'Paddy from Cork' and 'Behold how Brightly'. An Irishman with 2000 scars across his back and two years' solitary confinement behind him danced a hornpipe. Then came James Porter's turn: standing, he gave his audience 'The Light Irishman'. Then there were sports, and finally fireworks, also paid for by the captain, and then bed, to which every man on the island 'peaceably returned', recalled Thomas Cook, 'even though there were boats in the harbour'.

It was a bizarre and dreamlike interlude in the lives of men accustomed to cruelty and hard labour, and one which could not last. Captain Maconochie had skated blithely over the difficulties of extending the Marks system to the Old Hands and they had believed him. The captain knew that later that year, the British parliament would take its first legislative step towards the abolition of transportation in New South Wales. What he had failed to acknowledge, however, was that for those already in Australia and already in the system, this historic legislation would make no difference. Whatever he told them, the ship thieves and their 1200 Kingston hut mates were still there for the terms dictated by their sentences—those passed at home months, years or decades ago and any others passed since for re-offending in the colony. The act about to be passed thousands of miles away in London would change nothing for them. Far more important was the decision just taken in Sydney by Governor Gipps of New South Wales, Maconochie's immediate superior.

When Gipps had been informed of his subordinate's actions on Norfolk Island, he was alarmed. A letter from his office had been sent to the captain requesting that the old regime be reinstated in Kingston and the Marks system be confined, as agreed, to those at Longridge. Maconochie had ignored it. When further reports reached Sydney of partying convicts, fireworks and free liquor, Gipps found himself in a similar dilemma to that earlier suffered by Sir John Franklin in Hobart. Personally, he felt some sympathy with Maconochie's aims but the hostility of the mainland 'respectables' was intense. When celebrations of the royal birthday were reported, 'the feeling against him', Gipps wrote to London, 'was analogous to that which, a dozen years ago, manifested itself in the West Indies against any attempt to ameliorate the condition of slavery'. Unequivocal orders were sent to re-apply the old system to the Old Hands.

On 18 July, three months after Maconochie's speech, this decision was sadly relayed to the men on Norfolk Island. The hopes irresponsibly aroused by their new commandant were diminished. It seemed the abolitionists in the British parliament would do nothing for them. Once more, minds turned to escape by any means possible.

Off Norfolk was a rock with a name that awoke Macquarie memories: Phillip Island. It had no permanent dwellings but officers used to go there often with their tents and cooking pots for a few days' hunting and relief from duty, rowed over and brought back by a convict crew. 'Some few months after they were transferred [back] to the Old System', wrote Thomas Cook, six convicts went to fetch two officers and a soldier from this small island, together with their 'fire arms and ammunition' (kept in a carpetbag), 'tent clothing and a small quantity of provisions'. Lacking the training of Macquarie Harbour guards, the soldiers handed their carpetbag, provisions and canvas to the convicts in the boat before getting in themselves. Worse, they overlooked the fact that one of the convicts had moved to the stern, where the loaded guns had been put. 'That which followed,' said Thomas Cook, 'was certain to happen. They lost the boat and I believe not one Old Hand in 100 so circumstanced would have disregarded similar facilities for escape.' Of course the alarm was eventually raised but by then the stolen boat was out of sight. For the next fortnight, a strong south-easterly breeze blew. The stolen vessel was uncovered and there were thousands of miles of open water to cover to the north before the fugitives hit land. 'It was the general opinion,' Cook said, 'that they met with Watery Graves.'

Soon after this escape, one 'prisoner Lynch' was found absent from muster. A search of the boats discovered that he had arranged to have himself 'nailed into a packing box and sent to Sydney'.

Then came another attempt at ship-thievery that had odd echoes. In 1841, James Porter had been appointed cox to a boat crew off

Cascades. Charles Lyon, his equal in seamanship and experience, was an obvious candidate for a similar post on some other government boat—if he had not been one of the two Vandemonians believed to have met 'Watery Graves' on the boat seized off Phillip Island. James Porter and one other crew member of the second stolen boat, Thomas Cook recalled, 'had been acquainted . . . in the Penal Colony of Van Diemen's Land from which Latter place each had made his escape and had subsequently been convicted in England under fictitious names'. However, when the boat was seized off Cascade, the cox refused to go. When the other Vandemonian convict got away, it was James Porter who gave the alarm and started the pursuit.

Whatever plans for escape the others were involved in, James Porter, for the first time in his life, was not interested in bolting. Withdrawal of the Marks system had been a severe blow but he still saw possibilities under the new regime that made it preferable to another stolen boat on another dangerous sea. Not all the captain's changes had been forbidden by Governor Gipps; indeed, even without the application of the Marks system, Maconochie's regime was radical and, for the hostile free on the mainland, still unacceptably soft on convicts. Among the ideas for reformation allowed to continue was a category of practices which did not then have a name, but has since acquired one: therapy.

Before leaving Sydney, the captain had submitted a list of materials he thought would be useful in his care of the islanders which raised eyebrows to the hairline at Government House. He wanted an encyclopaedia and cookbooks, narratives of travel and discovery, *Captain Cook's Voyages* and copies of *Robinson Crusoe*, tales of English history and anthologies of poetry, books to hearten the Irish (Maria Edgeworth) and the Scottish (Walter Scott); the plays of Shakespeare and, the only conventional request, dozens of Bibles. To complement this library, he wanted the raw materials of an orchestra: trumpets, horns, drums and two accordions, music paper for the copying of scores and a baton. Despite Gipps's veto of the Marks system, these materials were sent to Norfolk Island and placed at the Old Hands' disposal.

The scheme that appealed to the stunted talents of James Porter was the most potentially subversive of all. Literacy was a tool of revolution. It was the charge of 'writing on small pieces of paper' that had told against Porter on board the *Sarah*. At other labour camps, a man could get 100 lashes for trying to smuggle a letter out and a month in solitary for possession of a piece of writing paper. Defying all this, Maconochie had decided that reams of the stuff be made available to those who wished to write down and clarify their past. In so doing, he hoped they might rethink their future.

Thus in 1841, under Maconochie's eccentric gaze, James Porter wrote a second, fuller account of the events that had brought him to Norfolk Island. With the noose no longer over his head, defence was not his principal narrative object. In the pages that have survived, he dwells on his misspent youth and adventures with a few of the conventional nods to penitence expected of a man in his situation and mentions, wherever he can work them in, those who should have helped him do this, should not have let him do that, could have kept him on the straight and narrow if only they had done the other. There are equally frequent anecdotes shoehorned in of his own prowess in scrums, dealings with the ladies, bravery at sea and a few outrageous claims of Robin Hoodery. When he turned to the taking of the *Frederick*, there were no more protestations that he did not know what was being plotted, nor that he had been coerced into joining the mutineers. In this longer version, James Porter states he had been a principal planner and mover in the affair: 'I hit on a plan,' he wrote, 'to get rid of 2 soldiers and McFarlane by persuading the Sergeant to go and ask the Whale Boat to go fishing.' When they had gone,

'I asked the other two soldiers to come down the forecastle to hear some singing'. When the signal for action had been given, 'I ordered the mate and soldier to go below'.

The couple of pages allotted at the end of this manuscript to his life on Norfolk Island mention none of his old companions, not even his mate Billy Shires. Indeed Shires, now a tired old man in his forties, fades at this point from the records. He may have gone head down into the obscurity of good behaviour, too weary after decades of punishment to contemplate another adventure and its consequences, content to work his allotment and break his communal bread in anonymity; he may simply have been in a different mess and barracks from Porter, separated by new routines and new acquaintanceships. The presumed dead Lyon and Cheshire, if he was still on the Island, were no longer among Porter's concerns. Instead, there is a eulogy to the captain, partly a matter of form, but partly sincere. Porter's words of devotion were echoed by the other convicts who wrote their memoirs while on Norfolk Island. Accustomed to indifference, severity or contempt, they appreciated the sincerity of Maconochie's wish to give a future back to those in his care, however irresponsible he had been in promising what it was not in his power to promise. Porter wrote:

> His whole study has been to make us prisoners comfortable and by kind and Humane treatment to work a reformation in us.
>
> It has had the desired effect on many refractory Characters that could not be ruled by harsh and cruel treatment. I speak for myself and five more young men that would rush upon the points of Bayonettes to obtain our liberty previous to the Captain's arrival on the island, we have given our words not to abscond with a Boat, nor allow her to be taken under any circumstances. The Captain has placed dependence in us and we have proved to him . . . that our Commandant Humanity has brought

us to a sense of our duty, never to lose the only thing an exile doth
possess, his word.

After proving his reliability Porter was once again placed in a boat
crew, this time at the pilot-station of Cascade, the island's principal
landing place, where he reported to Mr Brown, the pilot, and lived
a life apart from the other Old Hands in Kingston. This was no less
a dangerous billet than at the Heads of Macquarie Harbour, with a
similar high incidence of death and injury. It also offered
opportunities to earn grace: in May 1841, Porter was involved in the
rescue of a boatload of officers who had carelessly gone fishing and
found themselves in danger when the winter weather closed in. For
this, he and the others who had risked their lives were described by
Captain Maconochie as being 'much in his confidence' and Porter's
life sentence was reduced to 14 years. It was a step along the one
escape route that he had not yet taken. 'I now live in hopes,' he
concluded piously that year in his memoirs, 'by my good conduct
of once more becoming a member of good Society.'

Not all Old Hands joined him in this resolve. In June 1842, the
brig *Governor Phillip* was on one of her regular runs from Sydney.
A group of 12 Old Hands manned the whaleboat which took
supplies to where she was anchored, overpowered her guard and, for
a desperate half-hour, commanded the brig. When the military rallied,
five of the convicts were shot and the rest captured and brought on
shore to be handed over to Captain Maconochie. They were in gaol,
awaiting sentence, when the next supply brig from Sydney, the
Lunar, was glimpsed three weeks later through rough weather off
Cascade.

The *Lunar* was bringing provisions and a detachment of soldiers
to relieve the Norfolk Island guard of their unpopular duty. On
9 July 1842, she anchored briefly off Cascade and took on the pilot,

Mr Brown, but was forced to weigh when the wind veered and threatened to blow her onto the rocks. For three weeks, she could not re-approach the wind-battered Norfolk coast. Only on 28 July did she finally come within signalling distance (about six miles off) and communication between ship and shore was possible. It was, as Maconochie would write to the Colonial Secretary, an opportunity which 'allowed some of our men to behave with extraordinary courage and steadiness'.

James Porter, now employed on the Cascade boat crew, was among those who saw the signal 'distressed for water' raised by the *Lunar* on 28 July. A whaleboat was readied with casks but, with the wind blowing strongly from the west all that day and the next, it could not put out. Two days after the first distress signal, the wind was as strong as ever and the *Lunar* stood still further out to sea. Captain Maconochie, fearing the consequences of thirst aboard the crowded brig, assembled the men of the Cascade pilot-station and asked for volunteers to row the water-boat out. 'As I expected,' he wrote, 'very many offered, but I was compelled to select the skilful as well as the willing.' He 'fixed on 8', of whom James Porter and another man, James Harris, 'as the most experienced, were to take the principal charge'.

The captain was, of course, aware of the danger, as these were obviously 'circumstances of great temptation and delicacy': a repeat of those in which prisoners had attempted to take the *Governor Phillip* only a month ago. However, he had no free men to take charge of the convict-boat crew. The pilot was already aboard the *Lunar*, he 'scrupled greatly' to order on such a dangerous mission 'any married Man with a Family on the Island', which ruled out much of its free population; and the coxswain, Mr Hurley, although free, was 'a worn out man, become nervous through growing debility, and thus to have sent him would have very greatly increased the risk, coolness, in an open Boat in a Sea-way, being even more necessary than skill'.

Thus a full crew of convicts was chosen to ferry 70 gallons of water in small kegs through crashing seas to the *Lunar*. Their whaleboat could only be launched at high water, but when that came at half-past two, it was clear that there was not enough daylight left for them to reach the *Lunar* and return safely. Those aboard the Sydney brig would have to suffer another night. At first light the next day, the *Lunar* was made out about 14 miles off and the whaleboat was launched through the surf with orders from Maconochie to James Porter and James Harris that they were under no circumstances to go further than eight miles offshore, 'the utmost limit that the water was at all smoothed by the island'. Those left on land climbed the hill behind Ball's Bay to light fires designed to 'call [the brig's] attention, and engage her to approach', meeting the men rowing out. The plan misfired: the *Lunar*'s captain 'not thinking it possible that a boat could be sent in such weather', took the flames as a signal to stand off and the whaleboat, 'after a very severe pull', was forced to turn round eight miles out. At two, the oarsmen were back, the water-kegs unbroached. All were aware that the suffering aboard the *Lunar* must be severe, but they were left with no choice.

Captain Maconochie, waiting, wet, on the beach at Ball's Bay, knew it would be asking too much of men already tired and with another 'severe pull' before them to return the boat to the pilot-station at Cascade and bring her back round the headland the next day. Logic dictated that she and her oarsmen must stay that night in Ball's Bay, ready for another attempt in daylight; penal prudence, however, suggested otherwise, for in Ball's Bay, unlike Cascade, there was 'no establishment, nor Boat-Shed, and, consequently, we could take none of our usual precautions for [the boat's] safety'. Nevertheless, Maconochie took the decision to trust his eight men who, though exhausted, 'volunteered to haul [the whaleboat] off to a grapnel a considerable distance from the shore, and sleep in her', protecting the boat not only from the wind and surf, but also from any would-be fugitives creeping up from Kingston.

First light on Monday 1 August brought another crashing surf and the men aboard the *Lunar*, hovering within Maconochie's eight-mile limit, were astonished to see a whaleboat plunging towards them across the high waves. The grateful marines expressed their thanks in a 'subscription' for the eight oarsmen of £2 14s 'as an acknowledgement of the relief afforded by their courage and exertions to their Comrades on board the Brig'. The 70 gallons were enough to keep the company of the *Lunar* healthy until, a couple of days later, she was able finally to anchor in Cascade, much battered and with some miserably sick soldiers aboard.

The *Lunar* took a week to unload. When finally she was empty, her Master took stock of her condition and went to Captain Maconochie. 'If compelled to put to sea without the assistance that he required,' the captain reported, 'he would feel compelled to lodge a Protest against us, to secure himself from the probable consequences.' His vessel was again short of water, and wood, the crew was 'worn out and almost mutinous', he needed more ballast and the time and resources to carry out a few 'indispensable repairs'. For these, he wanted 'a Sail-Maker and Ship's Carpenter at least two days on board and a few Sailor Men besides, to assist in knotting and splicing his rigging, securing his Masts and stowing the Ballast and Water in his Hold'.

The mention of a possibly mutinous crew put Maconochie in an even more worried frame of mind than he had been before sending out the water-boat. Unhappy seamen and fugitive convicts were a nightmare combination. 'If the Crew were dissatisfied,' he pointed out, 'they might even offer to give up the Vessel to them.' He suggested the soldiers, but the Master said 'the Military were very much in the way on board . . . and knowing, as he now did, the men I would select, he would rather trust to them'. Eventually, Maconochie agreed. It was a second opportunity for James Porter and his mates to come forward and demonstrate their trustworthiness. From 7 to 10 August, they worked diligently aboard the *Lunar*, and 'landed', Maconochie said, 'as sober as they went on board, a circumstance the more remarkable as there was Liquor on board and neither the Mate nor the Crew . . . uniformly set them the same example'.

James Porter and his fellow convicts had behaved admirably and Captain Maconochie was determined they should receive some reward. On 4 October, his long, detailed description of events left the island addressed to the Colonial Secretary. This emphasised not only the 'animal courage' of the men involved but also their honesty, and recommended that 'the utmost may be done [for them] that His Excellency thinks in the circumstances can be granted'. As Maconochie reminded those on the mainland, 'a severe example of the consequences of misconduct is probably at this moment inevitable on the Island', for the men who had attempted to seize the *Governor Phillip* were still in gaol awaiting a sentence which all knew must be capital. 'A signal instance,' the captain suggested, 'of what may be hoped from good conduct occurring at the same time, would have an extremely good effect.'

Despite the reservations held on the mainland about Captain Maconochie's perceived softness on convicts, his narrative of events, supported by a letter from the Master of the *Lunar*, was persuasive. Among the recommendations adopted by the Colonial Secretary was that of reducing James Porter's sentence to seven years and transferring him to the mainland. The delays of transoceanic correspondence meant it was not until May 1843 that news of this pardon arrived. That month, Porter left the Island of Demons and, 'much worn out but steady and well conducted', was taken to Sydney. In that busy and prosperous city, among the thousands of convicts and ex-convicts younger, stronger and with greater reserves of energy than Porter, Police Number 324 finally slips from view.

Epilogue

If James Santiago Porter O'Connor disappeared from the archives, he did not quite disappear from Australian writing. As the man himself faded from view, a fictionalised alter ego emerged, a chirpy little phoenix arising from the ashes of Macquarie Harbour and Norfolk Island.

The original of Porter's first, brief memoir, written in 1837 while under sentence of death in Hobart gaol, had been archived among the records of the colonial government but not before it had been sent out into the world as a serialisation in the pages of the *Hobart Courier*. In 1841, Porter's second, much longer account was filed away as government property without any mention in colonial publications—the ship thieves of Macquarie Harbour were no longer news. It was the Hobart Gaol version that formed the basis of what popped up in 1844 on the other side of the world. Seven years after the trial in Hobart Town, a serialisation began in a provincial Scottish newspaper, the *Fife Herald*. It was entitled 'The Convict' and it purported to be the adventures of one James Connor. The following letter prefaced its first episode.

Sir

Having become possessed of some MS. notes written by a person named James Connor, a native of Dublin, giving a sketch of his sufferings in New South Wales, and in which there are a few stirring incidents, I have transcribed them. Should you consider the facts worthy of publication, you are welcome to them.

W.

'W' was David Wylie, an enterprising hack who offered an adventurous explanation for his possession of this convict memoir: he had not read it in a Vandemonian paper, nor had he been told of it by some official in the Colonial Office but claimed to come by it from a more exciting route. In his version, 'James Connor' had escaped from South America before the British came to get him, taken work aboard a Yankee ship and ended up in Bombay, where he bumped into an acquaintance. On being asked what he had been doing lately, 'Connor' handed a bundle of notes to the man which 'were given to [Wylie] by a brother of one of the officers of the vessel to which Connor's friend was attached'. As in Van Diemen's Land, the adventures of 'James Connor' and his gang proved so titillating that when their serialisation ended, they were printed as a book and sold at two shillings each to eager Scottish readers.

Three years later, Wylie, now writing under a whimsical Chinese version of his name, 'Y-Le', popped up in Montreal, Canada with *Recollections of a Convict and Miscellaneous Pieces,* a rehash of the Fife narrative dedicated to the 'Montreal Shakspeare [sic] Club'. This version dropped the story of Bombay and the Yankee ship but the author insisted nevertheless that it 'must not be looked upon as fiction' and that 'the incidents . . . were recounted to me by parties conversant with the facts'.

Wylie's versions of the ship thieves' story, necessarily based on the account left by just one of them, began the creation of James Porter's fictional avatar. The role in which he had cast himself when writing in Hobart gaol—decent chap caught up in events beyond his control, restraining the violence of others—was taken up and reinforced. David Wylie's 'James Connor' had to be coerced into joining the mutiny and eventually did so only 'on condition that no blood is shed, for my hands have never yet taken the life of a fellow-being and, horrid as our condition has been, I, for one, will not consent to the taking away of life'. It was a poetic rendition of Porter's own defence to the many and various courts he had faced during his life: they made me! It wasn't me! I didn't want to!

After David Wylie had milked his story in Scotland and Canada, it lay unnoticed for three decades. The abolitionists had won, convictry had ended and the Australian territories were burying their nastinesses out of sight. Australia was no longer the fatal shore, but the lucky country and tales of brutality and hardship were not popular. Then, in 1874, came publication of a book by Marcus Clarke, a succès de scandale which forced the past on the notice of the unwilling.

For the Term of his Natural Life, often described as the first Australian novel, is the long, unwieldy tale of John Rex, a good man transported for a crime he did not commit. When Rex is sent to Macquarie Harbour, he leads a group of mates in the capture of a ship and a voyage to freedom. It is a stirring episode and Marcus Clarke had done his homework in the Hobart archives to get the details right: whole sentences of the chapter describing the seizure of the fictional *Osprey* come straight from James Porter's pen. However, Clarke has fudged the characters and actions Porter described, allotting bad deeds to those whom his narrative required to be villains and good ones to those who must turn out the heroes, with the requirement that the fictional John Rex should be leading the action. It is Rex, not Billy Shires, who assures the officers that they can come up from the cabin without fear of violence; Rex, not John Barker, who tells the captain that he is in charge of the brig and, 'with these brave fellows, I'll take her round the world'; Rex who proposes 'that we divide the provisions. There are five of them and twelve of us. Then nobody can blame us', although Clarke does have them 'urged by self-interest, as well as sentiment, to mercy'. William Cheshire is turned from the 'weak lad' to an excitable, gun-toting figure, who calls, 'with a savage delight', for 'three cheers for old England and Liberty!', shoots one of the sentries dead and would have shot another had not he been restrained.

And James Porter? Where Wylie's 'James Connor' had been a man of action, as well as one of virtue, Clarke's 'James Porter' was a timid, rather spineless soul, bundled along by more vigorous others. His 'courage', wrote Clarke, 'was none of the fiercest' and he had 'for years [been] given over to that terror of discipline which servitude induces'. The actions and initiatives which Porter had claimed for himself in his own narratives are assigned by Clarke to others: it is not he whose singing holds the soldiers spellbound in the fo'c'sle; when the signal comes, he does not rush forward but is 'ordered' by Rex to guard the fo'c'sle hatch and makes such a poor job of it that one of the soldiers escapes.

If Porter ever read *For the Term of his Natural Life*—and he may have been still alive in 1874, although an elderly man—he must have smiled wryly. The Hobart gaol narrative may have helped save his neck by depicting him as an innocent but it did little to substantiate his later ebullient presentation of himself as leader and devil-may-care adventurer. At a distance of fourteen decades, it is impossible to ask the real James Porter to step forward. Wylie's character, however, has disappeared among the tens of thousands of slightly written adventure stories thrown up by empire. *For the Term of his Natural Life* is considered an Australian classic. If James Porter has an epitaph, it is in Marcus Clarke's story of the *Osprey*—and surely not what the little cockerel himself would have chosen.

A Note on Sources

Unpublished primary sources:

James Porter's two manuscripts are held in the Dixson Library, Sydney. Correspondence between Governor Arthur and the British Colonial Office is held in the British National Archive (CO 280 and CO 408), as is correspondence between the British Consul General in Chile and the British Foreign Office (FO 16) and documents relating to the voyage of the *Sarah* (Transportation Register in HO 11 and Surgeon's Report in ADM 101).

Documents relating to HMS *Blonde* and other British vessels in South America are in the British National Archive (ADM 53). Records of courts martial are in National Archive records WO 91 (British army) and ADM 1 (British Royal Navy).

Newspapers consulted include the *Fife Herald*, the *Tasmanian* and the *Colonial Times*.

Published primary sources:

The letters and works of James Backhouse, *The Exile's Lamentation* by Thomas Cook, *For the Term of His Natural Life* by Marcus Clarke, the works of Alexander Maconochie, *Notes of an Exile to Van Diemen's Land* by Linus Miller, Robert Fitzroy's *Narrative*.

Primary sources published on the web:

1838 British Parliamentary Report on Transportation, Decisions of the Nineteenth Century Tasmania Courts, *The Voyage of the Beagle* by Charles Darwin.

Principal secondary sources:

Sarah Island and *Macquarie Harbour Historical Research* by Ian Brand, *Great convict escapes by convicts in colonial Australia* by Warwick Hirst, Charles Bateson *The Convict Ships*, Robert Hughes *The Fatal Shore*, Ian Duffield *From Slave Colonies to Penal Colonies, Chain Letters: Narrating Convict Lives*, ed Lucy Frost and Hamish Maxwell-Stuart.

Acknowledgements

Tom Rees; Tristan Palmer; Lisa Highton, Vanessa Radnidge and Deonie Fiford at Hachette Livre Australia; the staff of the Dixson Library and the Mitchell Library, Sydney; the State Library of Tasmania; the National Library of Australia, Canberra; the British Library, London and the National Archive, London.

Picture Acknowledgements

Note: The pictures throughout the text are representative of the life and times of James Porter. No known images exist of him or his fellow ship thieves.

Picture section one:

Page 1 Portrait of a Convict (artist Peter Gordon Fraser), Allport Library and Museum of Fine Arts, State Library of Tasmania.

Page 2 *Top*: Prison-ship in Portsmouth Harbour (Edward William-Cooke, 1811-1880) nla.pic-an9058453, National Library of Australia. *Bottom*: Hobart Town, Van Diemen's Land (R. G. Reeve, 1811-1837) nla.pic-an6016427, National Library of Australia.

Page 3 *Top*: Flogging prisoners, Tasmania (James Reid Scott, 1839-1877) nla.pic-an6332106, National Library of Australia. *Bottom*: Chain gang. Convicts going to work nr. Sidney [sic] (Edward Backhouse), Allport Library and Museum of Fine Arts, State Library of Tasmania.

Page 4 *Top*: The chain gang mustered after the day's work (Frederick Mackie, 1812-1893) nla.pic-an4767719, National Library of Australia. *Bottom*: The settlement at Macquarie Harbour (Thomas Lempriere), Tasmaniana Library, State Library of Tasmania.

Page 5 *Top*: The Gates, Macquarie Harbour (Thomas Lempriere), Tasmaniana Library, State Library of Tasmania. *Bottom*: New sawpits, Macquarie Harbour (Thomas Lempriere), Allport Library and Museum of Fine Arts, State Library of Tasmania.

Page 6 Governor Arthur (W. Macleod), Tasmaniana Library, State Library of Tasmania.

Page 7 *Top*: Phillip Island from the N.W. extremity to the overseer's hut, Macquarie Harbour (Thomas Lempriere), Allport Library and Museum of Fine Arts, State Library of Tasmania. *Bottom*: Mewstone, bearing S.S., as seen from the vessel between the rock and the land (Thomas Lempriere), Tasmaniana Library, State Library of Tasmania.

Page 8 Map by Pigs Might Fly Productions.

Picture section two:

Page 1 *Top*: Wreck of the *Waterloo* convict ship, Cape of Good Hope, 28th August 1842, Allport Library and Museum of Fine Arts, State Library of Tasmania. *Bottom*: 'Wreck' by Haughton Forest, Allport Library and Museum of Fine Arts, State Library of Tasmania.

Pages 2–3 Map by Pigs Might Fly Productions.

Page 4 *Top*: Sailing ship near entrance to harbour (Charles-Claude Antiq, b. 1824), nla.pic-an3281048, National Library of Australia. *Bottom*: *Trachten von Concepcion*, Traditional costumes from Concepcion (1840), courtesy Philographikon, Germany.

Page 5 Map by Pigs Might Fly Productions.

Page 6 *Top*: Perilous situation of the boat *Maeander* at the bar, Norfolk Island (1856), nla.pic-an9455517, National Library of Australia. *Bottom*: Norfolk Island, the convict system (1847) nla.pic-an8934779, National Library of Australia.

Page 7 James Porter manuscript, poem, courtesy Dixson Library, State Library of New South Wales.

Page 8 Sydney Cove (John Skinner Prout, 1805-1876) nla.pic-an6940079, National Library of Australia

Index

Praise for *The Floating Brothel*

'This wonderfully vivid book, beautifully written and all
the more enthralling for being historically accurate, will stay in
my mind for many months.' *Daily Mail*

'Siân Rees wears her considerable learning lightly, and there is not a dull
moment in what is ... a wonderfully earthy read.' *Guardian*

'Rees uses smells, sights, and sounds as sensitively as a locksmith
uses keys to prise open a Georgian world in some ways surprisingly
like our own, in others almost imaginably different. Her accounts of public
executions, or communal childbirth in a tent on deck after nine months at
sea, have the immediacy of eyewitness testimony. So does her almost poetic
evocation of unwashed clothes, bodies and bedding and the stinking bilge in
a ship's hold...' *Daily Telegraph*

'...her writing really comes to life when she describes the experience of
sailing the high seas.' *Mail on Sunday*

'Hypnotising and utterly charming.' *Focus*

'... some of her maritime passages, with their accurate detail and
terminology, are up in the Patrick O'Brian class.... ...this book is quite an
achievement, and is to be highly recommended for its freshness and vigour.'
Literary Review

'Rees uses every scrap of information she can muster to produce a lively,
vibrant sense of these women as they must have lived their lives. ... This
outstanding debut sheds light on a fascinating, dark corner of history.'
Publishers Weekly Starred Review

'Rees debuts with a cracking tale...Historical writing of the first rank,
graphic and of real presence.' *Kirkus*

And not one friend to so

Too true I know that m

A heavy portion's fallen

With anguish full my

Far from my friends by

The feathered race wit

Extend their throats w

With Liberty they spri

While I a wretched Ca

Farewell my Sister, Ag

re long my glass of li